MW01489584

DON'T GIVE THE ENEMY A SEAT AT YOUR TABLE

Victory In Spiritual Warfare
(Christians, Demonization, & Deliverance)

Charles W Morris

Books may be ordered through booksellers or by
contacting:
RSIP
Raising the Standard International Publishing L. L. C.
https://www.rsipublishing.com

RSIP-Charles Morris
https://www.rsiministry.com
Navarre, Florida

ISBN: 9781960641113
Printed in the United States of America
Edition Date: June 2023

Table Of Contents

Chapter 1
SPIRITUAL WARFARE:
CHRISTIANS, DEMONIZATION, &
DELIVERANCE

Introduction

Many of us have had experiences in spiritual warfare. Some more than others. The rest may have heard of it but have had no experience. Having experiences or the lack of experiences are not criteria for the basis of establishing Biblical truth. Where should our experiences concerning spiritual warfare be found when establishing true doctrine? When establishing true doctrine, all of our experiences must be found in the Old Testament's shadow and the New Testament's substance.

Harmful habits, negative thinking, and irrational feelings" may lead to sinful behavior and bondage, but rest assured, freedom is within reach.

In a world filled with unproductive, destructive, and harmful thoughts, it is all too easy to feel overwhelmed and trapped in a cycle of repeating mistakes. My goal in this book is to remind you that these thoughts are not of God but rather the insidious whispers of a lurking enemy—an evil force seeking to claim control over your life. With unwavering conviction, I urge readers to recognize and confront these falsehoods. God's Word offers a path toward restoring peace, rest, and authority over the thoughts and activity of the demonic.

1

Using God's Word, you can expose the endless cycle of destructive thinking and embrace practical Biblical guidance to recapture your emotions and break free from the chains that hold you captive. What is the true purpose behind the journey of facing challenging circumstances? When exercising Biblical faith, you are empowered to embrace trials and find meaning amidst the struggle.

The key lies in the battle for the mind. I present readers with powerful warfare Scriptures that shatter the powers of darkness and unleash God's abundant blessings and favor. With a prayerful approach to spiritual warfare, we will introduce biblical principles that will equip us to overcome demonic influence and oppression.

How much from God's Word have you studied concerning spiritual warfare? What does it mean for you to put on the whole armor of God? When our Lord told us to cast out demons, was that limited to first-century Christians? No, all believers are called to cast out demons.

Is spiritual warfare limited to a unique gifting or calling among believers? No, all believers are called to engage in spiritual warfare. Could you have unknowingly given the enemy a seat at your table? How can we have and maintain victory in spiritual warfare? What does the Bible say about Christians, demonization, and deliverance?

You may have heard differing opinions concerning demonic activity in the life of people, especially in the lives of Christians. Let me say that there are a lot of differing opinions about whether a Christian can have a demon or not. What does the Word say about this? There are differing opinions, but the Word of God should be consulted for the answer.

What examples from the Bible can we draw upon to understand the teaching of demonic activity? The Bible provides examples of Jesus and His disciples casting out demons. How can the demonic affect you as you seek to walk with the Lord? What authority do you have when it comes to dealing with demons? What authority do you have in helping others who feel they have a spiritual demonic stronghold? Believers have the authority to help others through prayer, deliverance, and the power of the Holy Spirit.

Is spiritual warfare a spiritual gift or a mandate for all believers? These questions and many more will be addressed in this teaching.

- Some would say that only lost people can have a demon.
- Some would say that a Christian with the indwelling Holy Spirit (Holy Spirit within) but who has not been baptized with the Holy Spirit can have a demon.
- Some would say that a Christian with the indwelling Holy Spirit (Holy Spirit within) and baptism with the Holy Spirit (Holy Spirit upon) can have a demon.
- Some would say the demonic has no right or authority in the life of a believer.
- Some would even go so far as say they believe all demons are already judged and cast into hell. Therefore, we cannot be tempted by the demonic.

My, my. With all these differing viewpoints, how can we arrive at the truth? Simple. Let's let the Word interpret the Word without our denominational bias, experiences, or our lack of experiences dictating Scriptural doctrine.

But what does the Word of God say? We hope to clear this up in this study. This study guide and workbook will equip you with the necessary tools to navigate the spiritual warfare that infiltrates our lives. This warfare training is a transformative journey of canceling the lies that threaten to wreck your life and allows you to embrace life fully alive in Christ.

In order to do this, I cannot just give a yes or no answer about Christians being "demonized" without laying a foundation to build on. Do you want to be free? Your freedom is not based on my opinions or the opinions of others. Your freedom rests completely on your faith in God's Word, the finished work of our Lord Jesus Christ, and the ministry of the Holy Spirit. We can be as free as we want to be. In fact, let me take it a step further. We are at this moment as free as we want to be. The Father is not holding us back from our spiritual, mental, emotional, and relational freedoms. It is our faith and choices. We all will do everything today that we deem necessary to us. Time and choices are not our enemies. What we do with our time and choices becomes our strengths, victories, or defeats.

"Don't Give the Enemy a Seat at Your Table" will address demonization in and through a believer and the authority of what Satan and the demonic can and cannot do in our lives.

I have seen and, sadly to say, been a part of extremes on both sides of the fence in this theological debate of the possibility of a Christian having the unfortunate ability to have a demon. So, join me, and let's tear down and root out so we can build upon a proper foundation.

Questions For Chapter 1

1. How should we establish true doctrine when it comes to spiritual warfare?

2. Was casting out demons limited to first-century Christians?

3. Is spiritual warfare limited to a unique gifting or calling among believers?

4. What examples from the Bible can we draw upon to understand the teaching of demonic activity?

5. What authority do believers have in helping others with spiritual demonic strongholds?

Chapter 2
THE "DON'T ASK, DON'T TELL" APPROACH CONCERNING DEMONS

Some take the extreme on one side, stick their heads in the sand, and deny the current existence or activity of demons. If you are one of these people, then know a demonic spirit is deceiving you. Therefore, my perspective on people who deny the existence or activity of demons is that they are being deceived by a demonic spirit and are blinded to the truth.

Rejecting the current activity of the demonic could mean that your eyes are blinded, and you are dull of hearing concerning truth. If this offends you, you will most likely not continue reading this study guide on spiritual warfare. It is interesting that people can so quickly discard the message that would set them free.

I have had Christians tell me not to speak about demons around them because they take an "out of sight, out of mind" attitude. In other words, they believe if they don't speak about demons or bother demons in any way, then the demons will not bother them. This thought pattern is demonic and an extremely dangerous position because the demons don't care if we believe in them or not. Their activity around us is not dictated to nor hindered by our ignoring them as though they don't exist.

The more people joke about demonic activity and pretend demons are nothing more than religious scare tactics, are revealing the enemy already deceives them. The most significant problem with deception is that people don't realize they are deceived. Deception is deceivingly deceptive. Look what the Apostle Paul says about how people will act and react in the last days.

> ***2 Timothy 3:1-7 (ESV) But understand this, that in the last days there will come times of difficulty. 2 For people will be lovers of self, lovers of money, proud, arrogant, abusive, disobedient to their parents, ungrateful, unholy, 3 heartless, unappeasable, slanderous, without self-control, brutal, not loving good, 4 treacherous, reckless, swollen with conceit, lovers of pleasure rather than lovers of God, 5 having the appearance of godliness, but denying its power. Avoid such people. 6 For among them are those who creep into households and capture weak women, burdened with sins and led astray by various passions, 7 always learning and never able to arrive at a knowledge of the truth.***

Good Christian people will be persecuted, while bad people become worse in character and lifestyle as they are deceiving people while they are themselves being deceived.

> ***2 Timothy 3:12-13 (ESV) Indeed, all who desire to live a godly life in Christ Jesus will be persecuted, 13 while evil people and impostors will go on from bad to worse, deceiving and being deceived.***

However, rest assured that the cross and the blood of the Lamb shed for us are enough to defeat the enemy's schemes. You need to know that the enemy's plans are meant to be evil towards you. However, God has a plan to bless you.

Genesis 50:20 (ESV) As for you, you meant evil against me, but God meant it for good, to bring it about that many people should be kept alive, as they are today.

Psalms 119:71 (ESV) It is good for me that I was afflicted, that I might learn your statutes.

Questions For Chapter 2

1. What is the author's perspective on people who deny the existence or activity of demons?

2. Why does the author consider the attitude of "out of sight, out of mind" towards demons dangerous?

3. How does the author describe the impact of deception?

4. According to 2 Timothy 3:1-7, what will people's behavior be in the last days?

5. How does the author reassure the readers regarding the enemy's schemes?

Chapter 3
KNOWING THE SCHEMES OF THE ENEMY

When it comes to the enemy's plans, did you know you don't need to be in the dark? Are you aware that you can be very strategic in your spiritual walk in possessing the gates of your enemies?

The enemy has devised plans against you. He roams about as a lion seeking those whom he can devour. You need to put on the armor of God and pray for God's wisdom. Why would you need armor unless you are in a battle? Putting on the whole armor of God refers to being prepared and equipped for spiritual warfare. You are to be aware of the plans of the enemy. You certainly can't do this if you place your head in the sand and ignore the enemy out of fear.

1 Peter 5:8-9 ESV Be sober-minded; be watchful. Your adversary the devil prowls around like a roaring lion, seeking someone to devour. (9) Resist him, firm in your faith, knowing that the same kinds of suffering are being experienced by your brotherhood throughout the world.

Luke 22:31-32 ESV "Simon, Simon, behold, Satan demanded to have you, that he might sift you like wheat, (32) but I have prayed for you that your faith may not fail. And when you have turned again, strengthen your brothers."

When exercising spiritual warfare, we must remember that Satan and the demons understand the concept of eternity and know their time to operate their schemes against mankind is short.

> *Revelation 12:12 ESV   Therefore, rejoice, O heavens and you who dwell in them! But woe to you, O earth and sea, for the devil has come down to you in great wrath, because he knows that his time is short!"*

Our Demonic Foes Are Not Toothless

Okay, I know that subtitle sounds silly. However, this is an example of the unbiblical statements I hear from people ignorant about spiritual warfare. One of the ways we can give the enemy a seat at our table is to have the false idea he is harmless.

Yes, I have heard that although the enemy roams about like a lion, we need not fear because God has pulled his teeth, and all he can do is gum us. I would love to see the Scriptures used for this false teaching. Maybe this makes for emotional preaching to incite a crowd with encouragement. However, it gives false assurance and opens us to demonic attacks from our spiritual enemies. The foolishness of this would be like inviting a rattlesnake into your bed at night and then believing you are perfectly safe.

Why would you need armor to do battle against a spiritual foe that is unarmed and harmless? Why are you called to put on the armor? Why would Peter warn us in 1 Peter 5:8-9 that Satan roams about like a roaring lion seeking whom he may devour? Peter tells us to be watchful and resist him in the faith. He also tells us he has caused the same suffering in Christian brothers worldwide. This activity does not sound harmless to me.

We are told to put on the armor to stand against the devil's schemes. The Scripture passage of Ephesians 6:11-12 does not sound like the enemy is toothless. Our fight is not fleshly but is in the spiritual realm. Therefore, we need to be clothed in our armor. Paul said that he fought a good fight. What is a good fight? A good fight is a fight that you win.

> **Ephesians 6:11-12 ESV Put on the whole armor of God, that you may be able to stand against the schemes of the devil. (12) For we do not wrestle against flesh and blood, but against the rulers, against the authorities, against the cosmic powers over this present darkness, against the spiritual forces of evil in the heavenly places.**

We need not be ignorant (unlearned and unaware) of the schemes and plans of the enemy. The Apostle Paul explaining one of the plans of the demonic, stated that forgiveness was vital in defeating the schemes of Satan. Therefore, let your spiritual warfare begin with forgiving those who have wronged you or in situations you perceive to have been wronged.

> **2 Corinthians 2:10-11 ESV (10) Anyone whom you forgive, I also forgive. Indeed, what I have forgiven, if I have forgiven anything, has been for your sake in the presence of Christ, (11) so that we would not be outwitted by Satan; for we are not ignorant of his designs.**

The enemy will and does disguise himself as an angel of light. Therefore, it is easy to call good evil and evil good if the enemy deceives us.

> **2 Corinthians 11:13-14 ESV (13) For such men are false apostles, deceitful workmen, disguising themselves as apostles of Christ. (14) And no wonder, for even Satan disguises himself as an angel of light.**

Questions For Chapter 3

1. What does it mean to put on the whole armor of God?

2. According to 1 Peter 5:8-9, what is one of the characteristics of the enemy described as a roaring lion?

3. Why does the author emphasize the importance of putting on the whole armor of God?

4. How does the author refute the notion that the enemy is toothless and harmless?

5. What does the author propose as a crucial element in defeating the schemes of Satan, according to 2 Corinthians 2:10-11?

6. How does Satan deceive people, as mentioned in 2 Corinthians 11:13-14?

Chapter 4
THE "DEMON BEHIND EVERY BUSH" APPROACH

W e know that the Lord called all of us into the deliverance ministry and to do spiritual warfare. What does John 14:12 emphasize about the demonic foes believers face? Believers in our Lord Jesus Christ are all called to cast out demons and resist the enemy. However, we should not become so "fixed" on one side of our Biblical mandate that we miss everything else the Father has called us to do. According to John 14:12, we are to do the works of our Lord.

> **John 14:12 ESV   "Truly, truly, I say to you, whoever believes in me will also do the works that I do; and greater works than these will he do, because I am going to the Father.**

I want to establish the foundational truths we need to know when dealing with the demonic. Is spiritual warfare a spiritual gift or a mandate for all believers? It is a mandate for all believers to engage in spiritual warfare and cast out demons

We must be assured of the Biblical mandate and authority we have been given to cast out demons. We are called to do the works that our Lord Jesus Christ did. For more on doing the works of Jesus, read my book, *"DOING THE WORKS OF JESUS."*

How did our Lord Jesus Christ cast out demons, according to the text in Matthew 8:16? Our Lord Jesus Christ cast out demons with a spoken word with authority. This truth is essential because I have seen people scream at demons like they were deaf. A simple spoken statement with authority will do far more than screaming when lacking anointing and authority. What authority do believers have when it comes to dealing with demons? Believers have authority in the name of Jesus to cast out demons. Remember, any authority we possess is of our Lord Jesus Christ and in His name.

> **Matthew 8:16 ESV That evening they brought to him many who were oppressed by demons, and he cast out the spirits with a word and healed all who were sick.**

Before receiving the indwelling Holy Spirit, who did our Lord Jesus Christ give authority to cast out demons? The disciples, who did not have the indwelling presence of the Holy Spirit, were given power and authority by the Lord Jesus Christ to cast out demons. Interestingly, all twelve of the disciples were sent out to fulfill the commands of our Lord Jesus. This number means Judas was with them as the disciples went out to minister. Judas was a believer at this point, like the other eleven, and was not yet filled with a demonic spirit. We know this because our Lord said Satan could not cast out Satan. A house cannot stand if it is divided against itself.

> **Matthew 10:1 ESV And he called to him his twelve disciples and gave them authority over unclean spirits, to cast them out, and to heal every disease and every affliction.**

Matthew 12:25-28 ESV *Knowing their thoughts, he said to them, "Every kingdom divided against itself is laid waste, and no city or house divided against itself will stand. (26) And if Satan casts out Satan, he is divided against himself. How then will his kingdom stand? (27) And if I cast out demons by Beelzebul, by whom do your sons cast them out? Therefore they will be your judges. (28) But if it is by the Spirit of God that I cast out demons, then the kingdom of God has come upon you.*

Our Lord cast out demons with just a spoken word and, in most cases, did not allow the demons to speak.

Mark 1:33-34 ESV *And the whole city was gathered together at the door. (34) And he healed many who were sick with various diseases, and cast out many demons. And he would not permit the demons to speak, because they knew him.*

One of the signs that follow a true believer in Christ is that they would cast out demons.

Mark 16:17 ESV *And these signs will accompany those who believe: in my name they will cast out demons; they will speak in new tongues;*

Luke 9:49-50 ESV *John answered, "Master, we saw someone casting out demons in your name, and we tried to stop him, because he does not follow with us." (50) But Jesus said to him, "Do not stop him, for the one who is not against you is for you."*

Read Luke 10:17-20 because you will find they are interesting Scriptures concerning spiritual warfare. First, we see that the 72 our Lord sent out had the tremendous authority to cast demons out of people. Even our Lord recognized the power in which the 72 operated. He encouraged them concerning the authority they exercised over the demonic.

I want to point out that this was before our Lord was crucified and raised from the dead. It was before John 20:22 when He commanded that they receive the Holy Spirit. As we do, these disciples did not have the indwelling Holy Spirit yet. However, they were still believers. Not only were they believers, but their names were written in heaven. This passage is vital for understanding the authority of a believer before the indwelling of the Holy Spirit, which was all those who believed before the resurrection of our Lord.

> *Luke 10:17-20 ESV The seventy-two returned with joy, saying, "Lord, even the demons are subject to us in your name!" (18) And he said to them, "I saw Satan fall like lightning from heaven. (19) Behold, I have given you authority to tread on serpents and scorpions, and over all the power of the enemy, and nothing shall hurt you. (20) Nevertheless, do not rejoice in this, that the spirits are subject to you, but rejoice that your names are written in heaven."*

Even those extremely religious yet spiritually lost and who have never known the Lord knew that deliverance ministry (casting out demons) was a discipline and mandate of the Christian faith. Our first-century believers and those who were religious yet lost understood demonization and deliverance.

Matthew 7:21-23 ESV "Not everyone who says to me, 'Lord, Lord,' will enter the kingdom of heaven, but the one who does the will of my Father who is in heaven. (22) On that day many will say to me, 'Lord, Lord, did we not prophesy in your name, and <u>cast out demons in your name</u>, and do many mighty works in your name?' (23) And then will I declare to them, '<u>I never knew you</u>; depart from me, you workers of lawlessness.'

So, we have established that we are called to cast out demons and be active in spiritual warfare. However, this can get out of balance. Some take the extreme and see a demon behind every bush. They attribute every problem in the Christian as demonic possession that can be fixed by deliverance. They become overly obsessed with demons, giving God a quick glance while giving the enemy an extended stare. We can become so excessively preoccupied with deliverance ministry that it could lead us to the mindset that demons are responsible for all sin within us.

This doctrine of blame or transference is extremely dangerous because it takes the responsibility for the Christian's choices and lifestyle away from him and causes him to say and believe that "the devil made me do it."

What is the danger of attributing every problem in a Christian's life to demonic possession? It diminishes the power of God in the person's life, denies personal responsibility for choices and lifestyle, and leads to an obsession with demons and neglect of God.

We know that according to the Word of God, we sin because of the lust of the heart. How can the demonic affect a person's walk with the Lord? The demonic can influence and tempt believers to sin. Any temptation the enemy gives us can only influence us because we already have that lust as a stronghold in the heart that can be preyed upon.

Example: I cannot be tempted to use a gun and go out and rob a bank. There is no lust in my heart that can allow the enemy to draw me into that area. I can name thousands of examples of things I cannot be tempted by because I know they are "not issues of my heart." However, I can name issues that are lusts of the heart that I still have to bring under authority and subjection to the Word of God and the power of God's Spirit. This discipline must be done until there are no longer lust issues in the heart. Some would easily say this is a demon, set up a deliverance session, and deny all personal responsibility. I know believers who move from deliverance session to deliverance session, hoping to be free without taking personal responsibility in dealing with a lustful heart.

> *James 1:13-15 ESV Let no one say when he is tempted, "I am being tempted by God," for God cannot be tempted with evil, and he himself tempts no one. (14) But each person is tempted when he is lured and enticed by his own desire. (15) Then desire when it has conceived gives birth to sin, and sin when it is fully grown brings forth death.*

> *James 4:1-4 ESV What causes quarrels and what causes fights among you? Is it not this, that your passions are at war within you? (2) You desire and do not have, so you murder. You covet and cannot obtain, so you fight and quarrel. You do not have, because you do not ask. (3) You ask and do not receive, because you ask wrongly, to spend it on your passions. (4) You adulterous people! Do you not know that friendship with the*

world is enmity with God? Therefore whoever wishes to be a friend of the world makes himself an enemy of God.

Genesis 8:21 ESV And when the LORD smelled the pleasing aroma, the LORD said in his heart, "I will never again curse the ground because of man, for the intention of man's heart is evil from his youth. Neither will I ever again strike down every living creature as I have done.

Jeremiah 17:9 ESV The heart is deceitful above all things, and desperately sick; who can understand it?

Questions For Chapter 4

1. How can the demonic affect a person's walk with the Lord?

2. What authority do believers have when it comes to dealing with demons?

3. Is spiritual warfare a spiritual gift or a mandate for all believers?

4. According to Mark 16, what is the sign/signs that follow a true believer in Christ?
   a) Speaking in new tongues
   b) Performing miracles
   c) Casting out demons
   d) All of the above

5. How did our Lord Jesus Christ cast out demons, according to Matthew 8:16?
   a) By screaming at them
   b) By using physical force
   c) By speaking a simple word with authority
   d) By praying for hours

Chapter 5
EVERYONE CAN'T BE RIGHT
CONCERNING DEMONIC ACTIVITY

Although these are extremes from both sides of the doctrine of spiritual warfare, after over forty-five years of ministry and experience, I can assure you they are not uncommon among the body of Christ. Somebody has to be wrong, and someone has to be right concerning the doctrine of demonization and spiritual warfare.

Everyone can't be correct concerning the operation of the demonic among believers. If God is not the author of confusion and He makes His Word clear through the leadership of the Holy Spirit and the revelation given to His Apostles and Prophets, it is time for sound teaching to be given in this area. We need to be able to fix our face like flint upon our heavenly Father and our Savior, the Lord Jesus Christ. While we stare intently at our Lord, we only need to glance at our enemy, knowing that he has already been defeated and his days are numbered.

Let us remember something that happened during a tragic era in our country. Our country experienced a civil war when a brother fought against a brother, and a friend fought against a friend. I want to point out that two years after the war ended, both sides were still battling and killing one another. The South lost the war and was defeated. Yet many were still armed and, in the field, fighting the Northern troops as if there was still a war to win.

21

Likewise, the devil and his demons were defeated when our Lord died on the cross, was buried, went into hell victorious, took the keys of sin, death, and the grave away from him, and then rose from the dead. The enemy being defeated and losing the war is one thing. The enemy knowing that his days are numbered is another thing. This revelation does not mean that the demons are sitting idle and powerless, waiting for the execution of their final judgment. Even though our Lord Jesus Christ has defeated them, the demonic host is still actively lying, deceiving, stealing, and tempting everyone that gives in to their deception and temptation. All lost people are children of the enemy. Therefore, they have a large army for us to stand against. But bless God; we have been given the victory.

Hebrews 2:14 ESV Since therefore the children share in flesh and blood, he himself likewise partook of the same things, that through death he might destroy the one who has the power of death, that is, the devil,

Matthew 16:19 ESV I will give you the keys of the kingdom of heaven, and whatever you bind on earth shall be bound in heaven, and whatever you loose on earth shall be loosed in heaven."

Revelation 1:17-18 ESV When I saw him, I fell at his feet as though dead. But he laid his right hand on me, saying, "Fear not, I am the first and the last, (18) and the living one. I died, and behold I am alive forevermore, and I have the keys of Death and Hades.

2 Thessalonians 3:3 ESV (3) But the Lord is faithful. He will establish you and guard you against the evil one.

Ephesians 6:16 ESV In all circumstances take up the shield of faith, with which you can extinguish all the flaming darts of the evil one;

Questions For Chapter 5

1. According to Hebrews 2:14, what did Jesus accomplish through His death?

2. What does Matthew 16:19 suggest about the authority given to believers?

3. In Revelation 1:17-18, what does Jesus declare about Himself?

4. What assurance is given in 2 Thessalonians 3:3 regarding believers' protection?

5. According to Ephesians 6:16, what role does the shield of faith play in relation to the evil one?

Chapter 6
WHO ARE THE "TRUE BELIEVERS"?

There is nowhere in the Bible explicitly saying that a Christian can have a demon. However, nowhere in the Bible does it explicitly state that a Christian cannot have a demon. Therefore, we should stop arguing from the position of silence. By now, if you are on one or the other side of the fence, the Ministry of Offense might be welling up within you. Let's look at what Jesus said in Matthew 11:6.

> ***Matthew 11:6 (ESV) And blessed is the one who is not offended by me."***

The term "offended" means tripped up or stumbling over. Sometimes when we become mentally and emotionally bonded to a belief or doctrine, we become unreachable and will fight to hold that belief to the end, no matter what evidence is presented. I presented a doctrine to a group of believers, and everyone saw it within the Scriptures except one gentleman. He argued that two famous pastors on TV and radio for over forty years had taught him his doctrine, which disagreed with what I taught. He was mentally and emotionally bonded to teaching from two men he loved and respected, and no matter what I taught from God's Word, he would not accept it unless it lined up with those two pastors. He recently left our fellowship to return to a group that taught as he believed. This man is an example of someone not having ears to hear. People believe everything you teach as long as you teach what they already believe.

Later, we will distinguish the difference between being demonized, oppressed, possessed, contaminated, or influenced by demonic spirits and what each means for us today. But as far as a Christian having a demon or not, the Word of God is silent. We would have trouble looking to a verse for clarification. We can take certain verses and make assumptions, but that is all they will be.

Some would say, "Pastor Charles, the Holy dwells in a believer; therefore, a demon cannot exist there." I hear you. However, there is a vast difference between the innermost man (my spirit), where the Holy Spirit dwells, and my inner man (my soul, how I think, feel, and choose), which I battle daily with sin. Through personal experiences, I have seen manifestations of demons in those who profess the Lord Jesus Christ. I've seen them leave the person whose life radically changes. Am I ready to make a theological teaching based on my experiences? No! I do not interpret the Scriptures based on experiences or lack of experiences. I judge all experiences or lack of experiences by the Word. If the Word is silent on my experience, I don't force the Word to agree. The experience is what it is. We should not make a hard-core doctrine out of it, build a fence around it, and tell people they must believe what we believe because we have experiences to prove it.

It is like the doctrine of the Trinity or the doctrine of the imminent return of our Lord Jesus Christ, known as the rapture. Although the word Trinity is not found in any Bible verse, the teaching can be found in the compilation of many Scriptures. Although "rapture" is not found in the Scriptures, it seems to be the "buzzword" of most sermons. When we don't have explicit Biblical texts substantiating some doctrines, the danger can be that we tend to start interpreting the isolated texts we have on the basis of our experiences or lack of experiences. We can also have a doctrinal belief passed on to us from family, friends, or our particular denominational church.

When we ask, "Can a believer have a demon?" we must first define the term "believer." There are believers in the Old Testament, believers during the Gospels, the believer on the cross, the believers in the room waiting right after our Lord Jesus rose from the dead, and the "after Pentecost" Acts chapter 2 believers. Once we identify the term "believer," we can take an honest look at demonic activity within the lives of believers.

Questions For Chapter 6

1. Does the Bible explicitly state whether a Christian can have a demon?

2. What does the term "offended" mean in Matthew 11:6?

3. Why is it important to distinguish between the innermost man (spirit) and the inner man (soul)?

4. Should theological teachings be based solely on personal experiences?

5. How does the lack of explicit biblical texts for certain doctrines pose a danger?

Chapter 7
THE OLD TESTAMENT BELIEVERS

In the Old Testament, from Adam in the Book of Genesis to the opening of the Gospels in Matthew, we have the stories of many people becoming believers. We need to abandon the idea that the Law is in the Old Testament and grace is in the New Testament. In that mindset, we say that Old Testament people became believers in God by the law. That is not true. They became believers of God by faith, just like the New Testament believers. However, they were under the law. When they placed their faith in the God of Abraham, Isaac, and Jacob, they had imputed righteousness placed on them. They were saved but could not go to heaven when they died. Their body went to the grave, but their soul and spirit went to Abraham's bosom, waiting for the promise of our Lord Jesus Christ.

We believe in the event that took place 2,000 years ago. Our early forefathers looked forward by faith and saw the event of the cross thousands of years before it happened. Nevertheless, these dear saints were saved and given grace by faith.

Romans 4:1-6 ESV What then shall we say was gained by Abraham, our forefather according to the flesh? (2) For if Abraham was justified by works, he has something to boast about, but not before God. (3) For what does the Scripture say? "Abraham believed God, and it was counted to him as righteousness." (4) Now to the one who works, his wages are not counted as a gift but as his due. (5) And to the one who does not work but believes in him who justifies the ungodly, his faith is counted as righteousness, (6) just as David also speaks of the blessing of the one to whom God counts righteousness apart from works:

Romans 4:9-22 ESV Is this blessing then only for the circumcised, or also for the uncircumcised? For we say that faith was counted to Abraham as righteousness. (10) How then was it counted to him? Was it before or after he had been circumcised? It was not after, but before he was circumcised. (11) He received the sign of circumcision as a seal of the righteousness that he had by faith while he was still uncircumcised. The purpose was to make him the father of all who believe without being circumcised, so that righteousness would be counted to them as well, (12) and to make him the father of the circumcised who are not merely circumcised but who also walk in the footsteps of the faith that our father Abraham had before he was circumcised. (13) For the promise to Abraham and his offspring that he would be heir of the world did not come through the law but through the righteousness of faith. (14) For if it is the adherents of the law who are to be the heirs, faith is null and the promise is void. (15) For the law brings wrath, but where there is no law there is no transgression. (16) That is why it depends on faith, in order that the promise may rest on grace and be guaranteed to all his offspring—not only to the adherent of the law but also to the one who shares the faith of Abraham, who is the father of us all, (17) as it is written, "I have made you the father of many nations"—in the presence of the God in whom he believed, who gives life to the dead and calls into existence the things that do not exist. (18) In hope he believed against hope, that he should become the father of many nations, as he had been told, "So shall your offspring be." (19) He did not weaken in faith when he considered his own body, which was as good as dead (since he was about a hundred years old), or when he considered the barrenness of Sarah's womb. (20) No unbelief made him waver concerning the promise of God, but he grew strong in his faith as he gave glory to God, (21) fully convinced that God was able to do what he had promised. (22) That is why his faith was "counted to him as righteousness."

In Hebrews 10:1-10 we clearly see that the Old Testament sacrificial system did not and could not take away sin. However, it pointed to the day the Son of God would shed His blood for the sinful human race.

Questions For Chapter 7

1. Were believers in the Old Testament saved by the law or by faith?

2. Where did the souls and spirits of Old Testament believers go when they died?

3. What does Romans 4:1-6 teach us about righteousness and faith?

4. What was the purpose of the Old Testament sacrificial system?

5. How did Abraham demonstrate his faith according to Romans 4:9-22?

Chapter 8
THE BELIEVERS WITHIN THE FOUR GOSPELS

Matthew, Mark, Luke, and John are interesting times. When we read these gospel narratives, we tend to think of the early church as it is today. Lest we forget, the Saints in the four Gospels were in the same condition as Old Testament saints. Our Lord Jesus Christ had not died on the cross yet. He had not risen from the dead, and His blood had not been spilled for the sins of mankind. What about those who believed in Christ before the cross and the resurrection of Christ? What did they have faith in and believe concerning the Messiah? Did they understand the complete picture of Christ dying on the cross for their sins?

The Saints in the four Gospels were saved the same way Old Testament saints were saved. They believed in God, and because of their faith, it was imputed unto them righteousness. They were still called believers and brothers. They were actually sent out to preach the gospel. However, sometimes, we miss the fullness of the gospel message. The Word says that John the Baptist came and preached the kingdom. The Word also says that our Lord Jesus Christ came and preached the kingdom. Matthew chapter 16, three years into Jesus' ministry, He began to tell them about His death, burial, and resurrection. Think about this. The gospel of the three days, which consist of His arrest, crucifixion, burial, and resurrection, was not preached until His third year of ministry. So, what was the gospel message preached in the first three years? It was the gospel of the kingdom of heaven. The gospel of the kingdom of heaven is the rule and reign of God in the hearts and lives of believers.

Therefore, the rule and reign of God in the hearts and lives of people, known as the gospel of the Kingdom of Heaven, was preached during His 3 ½ year ministry. The gospel of the Kingdom, among other things, healed the sick and cast out demons.

> **Matthew 3:1-2 ESV In those days John the Baptist came preaching in the wilderness of Judea, (2) "Repent, for the kingdom of heaven is at hand."**
>
> **Matthew 4:17 ESV From that time Jesus began to preach, saying, "Repent, for the kingdom of heaven is at hand."**
>
> **Matthew 4:23 ESV And he went throughout all Galilee, teaching in their synagogues and proclaiming the gospel of the kingdom and healing every disease and every affliction among the people.**
>
> **Matthew 9:35 ESV And Jesus went throughout all the cities and villages, teaching in their synagogues and proclaiming the gospel of the kingdom and healing every disease and every affliction.**
>
> **Matthew 24:14 ESV And this gospel of the kingdom will be proclaimed throughout the whole world as a testimony to all nations, and then the end will come.**

Our Lord began to preach the gospel of His death, burial, and resurrection around His third year of ministry. So, His three-day ministry was preached after He preached the gospel of the Kingdom for three years. Almost half of our Lord's supernatural events and major teachings happened in the last 6 to 8 months of His life. These events would include everything after Matthew 16:21, Mark 8:31, Luke 9:22, and John 7:2.

> **Matthew 16:21 ESV From that time Jesus began to show his disciples that he must go to Jerusalem and suffer many things from the elders and chief priests and scribes, and be killed, and on the third day be raised.**

> **Mark 8:31 ESV And he began to teach them that the Son of Man must suffer many things and be rejected by the elders and the chief priests and the scribes and be killed, and after three days rise again.**

> **Luke 9:22 ESV saying, "The Son of Man must suffer many things and be rejected by the elders and chief priests and scribes, and be killed, and on the third day be raised."**

What was the reaction of His disciples to this new message of His death? Let's look at Peter's response. He was part of the inner circle of three with our Lord.

> **Matthew 16:22 ESV And Peter took him aside and began to rebuke him, saying, "Far be it from you, Lord! This shall never happen to you."**

Now let's look at our Lord's response to the statement. Notice that it is not the Lord's response to Peter because He did not address Peter. He looks at Peter, but He addresses Satan himself. This passage should prove to be an interesting Scripture for us in light of the fact that Peter was a believer.

> **Matthew 16:23 ESV But he turned and said to Peter, "Get behind me, Satan! You are a hindrance to me. For you are not setting your mind on the things of God, but on the things of man."**

We know that Peter and the other disciples did not understand the whole truth of the work of the cross, yet they were saved because they had faith and believed that God would take care of their sin problem. The Holy Spirit was beside them but would one day soon dwell within them and then upon them. They didn't exactly know how God would accomplish the feat of settling their sin problem, any more than Adam, Abraham, Moses, or David knew how, but they believed God, and it was imputed unto them the righteousness of God. Look at Peter's statement of faith before Satan spoke through him.

> **Matthew 16:15-19 ESV He said to them, "But who do you say that I am?" (16) Simon Peter replied, "You are the Christ, the Son of the living God." (17) And Jesus answered him, "Blessed are you, Simon Bar-Jonah! For flesh and blood has not revealed this to you, but my Father who is in heaven. (18) And I tell you, you are Peter, and on this rock I will build my church, and the gates of hell shall not prevail against it. (19) I will give you the keys of the kingdom of heaven, and whatever**

you bind on earth shall be bound in heaven, and whatever you loose on earth shall be loosed in heaven."

Peter believed in Christ as the Son of the living God, and Jesus called him blessed for his faith and confession. Certainly, this is a saved man, as men were saved before the resurrection of Christ. However, in another instance, many of the disciples of Jesus (not the twelve) left as they found His teaching too challenging to accept. Here is the story from John 6:66-69.

> **John 6:66-69 ESV After this many of his disciples turned back and no longer walked with him. (67) So Jesus said to the Twelve, "Do you want to go away as well?" (68) Simon Peter answered him, "Lord, to whom shall we go? You have the words of eternal life, (69) and we have believed, and have come to know, that you are the Holy One of God."**

In John 6:66-69 we see the faith of Peter was common to the twelve. Peter said in verse 69, "and we have believed," speaking for all of the disciples. As to the receiving the indwelling of the Holy Ghost, this was another matter. It is only after John 20:22 that the Holy Ghost indwells all believers. The apostles lived through this transition period of knowing and believing in Christ without having the indwelling Holy Spirit until Christ was glorified, which we read in John 20:22. Consider the following verses.

> **John 7:38-39 ESV Whoever believes in me, as the Scripture has said, 'Out of his heart will flow rivers of living water.'" (39) Now this he said about the Spirit, whom those who believed in him**

were to receive, for as yet the Spirit had not been given, because Jesus was not yet glorified.

John 14:16-17 ESV And I will ask the Father, and he will give you another Helper, to be with you forever, (17) even the Spirit of truth, whom the world cannot receive, because it neither sees him nor knows him. You know him, for he dwells with you and will be in you.

Their salvation as believers by faith in God and His Word and their indwelling by the Holy Ghost occurred at two different times.

First, they believed in Him by faith.

John 2:11 ESV This, the first of his signs, Jesus did at Cana in Galilee, and manifested his glory. And his disciples believed in him.

Second, after our Lord Jesus Christ rose from the dead and was glorified, they received the indwelling of the Holy Spirit.

John 20:22 ESV And when he had said this, he breathed on them and said to them, "Receive the Holy Spirit.

It is clear from the Gospel of John that it is possible to believe by faith in Christ without understanding the reality of His resurrection. Several verses clearly show that when Jesus died, the disciples, who were already believers, as noted above, had not yet come to believe that He would resurrect from the dead. They thought all hope was lost.

Only after His post-resurrection appearances did they come to believe in His resurrection.

> *Luke 24:1-11 ESV But on the first day of the week, at early dawn, they went to the tomb, taking the spices they had prepared. (2) And they found the stone rolled away from the tomb, (3) but when they went in they did not find the body of the Lord Jesus. (4) While they were perplexed about this, behold, two men stood by them in dazzling apparel. (5) And as they were frightened and bowed their faces to the ground, the men said to them, "Why do you seek the living among the dead? (6) He is not here, but has risen. Remember how he told you, while he was still in Galilee, (7) that the Son of Man must be delivered into the hands of sinful men and be crucified and on the third day rise." (8) And they remembered his words, (9) and returning from the tomb they told all these things to the eleven and to all the rest. (10) Now it was Mary Magdalene and Joanna and Mary the mother of James and the other women with them who told these things to the apostles, (11) but these words seemed to them an idle tale, and they did not believe them.*

> *John 20:8-10 ESV Then the other disciple, who had reached the tomb first, also went in, and he saw and believed; (9) for as yet they did not understand the Scripture, that he must rise from the dead. (10) Then the disciples went back to their homes.*

Questions For Chapter 8

1. What was the primary message preached by Jesus during the first three years of His ministry?

2. When did Jesus begin to preach about His death, burial, and resurrection?

3. How did Peter initially react to Jesus' message about His death?

4. What did Jesus say in response to Peter's statement?

5. When did the disciples come to believe in the resurrection of Jesus?

Chapter 9
THE THIEF ON THE CROSS

hat about the thief on the cross? Not the thief that died in his sins. What about the thief that said, "Jesus, remember me when you come into Your kingdom." The Lord told the confessing thief, "Today you will be with me in Paradise." The blood of Jesus had been poured out for the sins of the world. While dying and knowing his time was almost finished, the thief placed his trust in the Lord Jesus Christ.

Do you think that it was easy for him to believe? He was staring at a man who was beaten, bloody, and gasping for every breath. The thief was placing His trust in a man with blood pouring from His head from the crown of thorns. The blood flowed from His beaten back, swollen face, and nail-pierced hands. His physical appearance didn't resemble someone who could save Himself, much less anyone else. Yet, the thief trusted Jesus with his soul. Again, his salvation would be like the salvation of Old Testament saints. He believed in God, and God imputed righteousness upon him. We know he became a believer because our Lord confessed that he would be with Him in paradise. Paradise is called Abraham's bosom and is the waiting place for all who had believed and died from Adam to that moment at the cross.

Luke 23:39-43 ESV One of the criminals who were hanged railed at him, saying, "Are you not the Christ? Save yourself and us!" (40) But the other rebuked him, saying, "Do you not fear God, since you are under the same sentence of condemnation? (41) And we indeed justly, for we are receiving the due reward of our deeds; but this man has done nothing wrong." (42) And he said, "Jesus, remember me when you come into your kingdom." (43) And he said to him, "Truly, I say to you, today you will be with me in Paradise."

Luke 16:22-31 ESV The poor man died and was carried by the angels to Abraham's side. The rich man also died and was buried, (23) and in Hades, being in torment, he lifted up his eyes and saw Abraham far off and Lazarus at his side. (24) And he called out, 'Father Abraham, have mercy on me, and send Lazarus to dip the end of his finger in water and cool my tongue, for I am in anguish in this flame.' (25) But Abraham said, 'Child, remember that you in your lifetime received your good things, and Lazarus in like manner bad things; but now he is comforted here, and you are in anguish. (26) And besides all this, between us and you a great chasm has been fixed, in order that those who would pass from here to you may not be able, and none may cross from there to us.' (27) And he said, 'Then I beg you, father, to send him to my father's house— (28) for I have five brothers—so that he may warn them, lest they also come into this place of torment.' (29) But Abraham said, 'They have Moses and the Prophets; let them hear them.' (30) And he said, 'No, father Abraham, but if someone goes to them from the dead, they will repent.' (31) He said to him, 'If they do not hear Moses and the Prophets, neither will they be convinced if someone should rise from the dead.'"

Questions For Chapter 9

1. What did the thief on the cross say to Jesus?

2. How did Jesus respond to the thief on the cross?

3. What was the physical condition of Jesus while the thief was placing his trust in Him?

4. How did the thief's salvation resemble the salvation of Old Testament saints?

5. What is Paradise referred to as in the context of the waiting place for believers who died before the cross?

Chapter 10
THE SPECIAL ROOM EXPERIENCE

Our Lord Jesus Christ had been raised from the dead and seen by a multitude of people. Some of the disciples were gathered together in a room. The Lord Jesus Christ walked into the room through the locked door. This testimony is recorded in John 20:20. The first word Jesus spoke was "peace," and then He made this proclamation. "Receive you the Holy Spirit." This statement was not a question or request but a command that could not be stopped. The disciples were already believers. They put their trust and faith in the Lord Jesus Christ and had imputed righteousness upon them, but they did not have the indwelling of the Holy Spirit.

Up to this point, the disciples were believers, just like Old Testament saints. When our Lord said, "Receive you the Holy Spirit," the Spirit of the living God came and dwelt within them, and they became believers like you and me today. This event was the first time a group had the indwelling of the Holy Spirit. This experience was to fulfill the command in John chapter 7 when our Lord Jesus Christ said the Holy Spirit is beside you, but one day He will be in you.

John 16:7 ESV Nevertheless, I tell you the truth: it is to your advantage that I go away, for if I do not go away, the Helper will not come to you. But if I go, I will send him to you.

John 7:37-39 ESV On the last day of the feast, the great day, Jesus stood up and cried out, "If anyone thirsts, let him come to me and drink. (38) Whoever believes in me, as the Scripture has said, 'Out of his heart will flow rivers of living water.'" (39) Now this he said about the Spirit, whom those who believed in him were to receive, for as yet the Spirit had not been given, because Jesus was not yet glorified.

John 14:16 ESV And I will ask the Father, and he will give you another Helper, to be with you forever,

John 15:26 ESV "But when the Helper comes, whom I will send to you from the Father, the Spirit of truth, who proceeds from the Father, he will bear witness about me.

John 20:19-22 ESV On the evening of that day, the first day of the week, the doors being locked where the disciples were for fear of the Jews, Jesus came and stood among them and said to them, "Peace be with you." (20) When he had said this, he showed them his hands and his side. Then the disciples were glad when they saw the Lord. (21) Jesus said to them again, "Peace be with you. As the Father has sent me, even so I am sending you." (22) And when he had said this, he breathed on them and said to them, "Receive the Holy Spirit.

Questions For Chapter 10

1. What did Jesus command the disciples when He appeared to them after His resurrection?

2. Were the disciples already believers before they received the Holy Spirit?

3. What did Jesus mean when He said the Holy Spirit would be "in" the disciples?

4. How did the disciples' experience of receiving the Holy Spirit fulfill the command from Jesus in John chapter 7?

5. In John 16:7, why did Jesus tell the disciples that it was to their advantage for Him to go away?

Chapter 11
THE UPPER-ROOM ACTS 2 BELIEVERS

The last group of believers would be known as the Acts chapter 2 believers. Our Lord Jesus Christ had risen from the dead, and He had been seen by a multitude of people numerous times. His commandment to the disciples was to go into the upper room in Jerusalem and wait until they were endued with power. They were waiting for the outpouring of the Holy Spirit. This group already had the Holy Spirit dwelling within them. They were Christians. The Acts chapter 2, believers were about to have the Holy Spirit fall upon them. It was to fulfill a prophetic word John the Baptist gave when he saw our Lord Jesus Christ at the beginning of His ministry. He said this man would baptize us in the Holy Spirit and with fire. When the Holy Spirit came within us at salvation, He baptized us into Christ and the body. These activities of bringing salvation and spiritual adoption were the work of the Holy Spirit. But it is not the Holy Spirit's job to baptize us with the Holy Spirit. After salvation, our Lord Jesus Christ's job is to baptize us with the Holy Spirit.

> *Matthew 3:11 ESV "I baptize you with water for repentance, but he who is coming after me is mightier than I, whose sandals I am not worthy to carry. He will baptize you with the Holy Spirit and fire.*

> *Luke 24:49 ESV And behold, I am sending the promise of my Father upon you. But stay in the*

city until you are clothed with power from on high."

Acts 1:4-5 ESV And while staying with them he ordered them not to depart from Jerusalem, but to wait for the promise of the Father, which, he said, "you heard from me; (5) for John baptized with water, but you will be baptized with the Holy Spirit not many days from now."

Acts 1:8 ESV But you will receive power when the Holy Spirit has come upon you, and you will be my witnesses in Jerusalem and in all Judea and Samaria, and to the end of the earth."

Acts 2:1-4 ESV When the day of Pentecost arrived, they were all together in one place. (2) And suddenly there came from heaven a sound like a mighty rushing wind, and it filled the entire house where they were sitting. (3) And divided tongues as of fire appeared to them and rested on each one of them. (4) And they were all filled with the Holy Spirit and began to speak in other tongues as the Spirit gave them utterance.

My Closing Thoughts About Biblical Believers

In the opening statements about Christians, we said there is nowhere in the Bible that says explicitly that a Christian can have a demon. There is nowhere in the Bible that says explicitly that a Christian cannot have a demon. The closest example we have is one minute Peter confessing Jesus is Lord and God, and the next minute Jesus is rebuking Satan in him.

Matthew 16:13 (ESV) Now when Jesus came into the district of Caesarea Philippi, he asked his disciples, "Who do people say that the Son of Man is?"

Matthew 16:15-17 (ESV) He said to them, "But who do you say that I am?" 16 Simon Peter replied, "You are the Christ, the Son of the living God." 17 And Jesus answered him, "Blessed are you, Simon Bar-Jonah! For flesh and blood has not revealed this to you, but my Father who is in heaven.

Matthew 16:21-23 (ESV) From that time Jesus began to show his disciples that he must go to Jerusalem and suffer many things from the elders and chief priests and scribes, and be killed, and on the third day be raised. 22 And Peter took him aside and began to rebuke him, saying, "Far be it from you, Lord! This shall never happen to you." 23 But he turned and said to Peter, "Get behind me, Satan! You are a hindrance to me. For you are not setting your mind on the things of God, but on the things of man."

We should not argue from Biblical silence. Therefore, we will approach this doctrine using only what we know to be Biblical. However, I do want to add this statement. The Bible does speak about believers having demons. The believers are those who trusted in God and had imputed righteousness before having the indwelling Holy Spirit, which started in John 20:22.

John 20:22 ESV And when he had said this, he breathed on them and said to them, "Receive the Holy Spirit.

It would be easy to believe that within the multitudes that came to our Lord Jesus Christ to receive deliverance, to find some who were believers. But just in case we find ourselves speaking from assumption or Biblical silence, in the next chapter, I would like to give some examples.

Questions For Chapter 11

1. What command from Luke 24:49 did Jesus give the disciples before the outpouring of the Holy Spirit?

2. Who is responsible for baptizing believers with the Holy Spirit?

3. What was the significance of the event in Acts chapter 2 for the believers?

4. How did the disciples' experience in Acts chapter 2 differ from their state before that event?

5. When did the indwelling of the Holy Spirit begin for believers, according to the Bible?

Chapter 12
BIBLICAL EXAMPLES OF BELIEVERS INFLUENCED BY DEMONIC SPIRITS (OLD TESTAMENT)

King Saul was influenced by demonic spirits. I want to take some liberty to build the case of who Saul was to God. In doing so, I need to go back to the birth of Samuel. Elkanah and his wife, Hannah, loved and served God, but Hannah did not give any children to her husband.

> *1 Samuel 1:8 (ESV) And Elkanah, her husband, said to her, "Hannah, why do you weep? And why do you not eat? And why is your heart sad? Am I not more to you than ten sons?"*

Hannah vowed that if God would open her womb and give her a son, she would give him back to the Lord to serve God all his life.

> *1 Samuel 1:11 (ESV) And she vowed a vow and said, "O LORD of hosts, if you will indeed look on the affliction of your servant and remember me and not forget your servant, but will give to your servant a son, then I will give him to the LORD all the days of his life, and no razor shall touch his head."*

The priest Eli saw Hannah weeping and praying and told her that God would grant her prayer request.

1 Samuel 1:17 (ESV) Then Eli answered, "Go in peace, and the God of Israel grant your petition that you have made to him."

Hannah conceived, fulfilling her prayers as Eli had spoken. She named the child Samuel.

1 Samuel 1:20 (ESV) And in due time Hannah conceived and bore a son, and she called his name Samuel, for she said, "I have asked for him from the LORD."

1 Samuel 1:27 (ESV) For this child I prayed, and the LORD has granted me my petition that I made to him.

To fulfill the vow, Hannah gave her only son Samuel to Eli, the priest to raise, and God started calling the young lad to follow Him to serve as a prophet of God to Israel.

1 Samuel 3:1 (ESV) Now the boy Samuel was ministering to the LORD in the presence of Eli. And the word of the LORD was rare in those days; there was no frequent vision.

1 Samuel 3:4 (ESV) Then the LORD called Samuel, and he said, "Here I am!"

1 Samuel 3:7 (ESV) Now Samuel did not yet know the LORD, and the word of the LORD had not yet been revealed to him.

1 Samuel 3:10 (ESV) And the LORD came and stood, calling as at other times, "Samuel!

Samuel!" And Samuel said, "Speak, for your servant hears."

1 Samuel 3:19 (ESV) And Samuel grew, and the LORD was with him and let none of his words fall to the ground.

Samuel became a mighty man of God, walking in the mantle of a Prophet before God to the nation of Israel. He called the people back to the Father's heart and told them to repent from their idolatry.

1 Samuel 7:3 (ESV) And Samuel said to all the house of Israel, "If you are returning to the LORD with all your heart, then put away the foreign gods and the Ashtaroth from among you and direct your heart to the LORD and serve him only, and he will deliver you out of the hand of the Philistines."

Samuel made his sons serve as Judges over Israel in his old age.

1 Samuel 8:1 (ESV) When Samuel became old, he made his sons judges over Israel.

The people cried out to Samuel for a King over them as the other nations had. God told Samuel to do it because they had rejected Him as their King.

1 Samuel 8:5-7 (ESV) and said to him, "Behold, you are old and your sons do not walk in your ways. Now appoint for us a king to judge us like all the nations." 6 But the thing displeased Samuel when they said, "Give us a king to judge us." And Samuel prayed to the LORD. 7 And the LORD said to Samuel, "Obey the voice of the people in all that they say to you, for they have not rejected you, but they have rejected me from being king over them.

Samuel, giving the people what they cried out for, prayed and searched for a king to serve over Israel. He found a man from the tribe of Benjamin named Saul.

1 Samuel 9:2 (ESV) And he had a son whose name was Saul, a handsome young man. There was not a man among the people of Israel more handsome than he. From his shoulders upward he was taller than any of the people.

The Lord told the prophet Samuel he would have a divine encounter with Saul the Benjamite.

1 Samuel 9:16 (ESV) "Tomorrow about this time I will send to you a man from the land of Benjamin, and you shall anoint him to be prince over my people Israel. He shall save my people from the hand of the Philistines. For I have seen my people, because their cry has come to me."

Samuel the Prophet anointed Saul as the King of Israel.

1 Samuel 10:1 (ESV) Then Samuel took a flask of oil and poured it on his head and kissed him and said, "Has not the LORD anointed you to be prince over his people Israel? And you shall reign over the people of the LORD and you will save them from the hand of their surrounding enemies.

And this shall be the sign to you that the LORD has anointed you to be prince over his heritage.

The Prophet Samuel tells Saul where he will go and what to do. In doing so, Saul would have a life-changing encounter with God. The Holy Spirit will fall upon him, and he will be a changed man.

1 Samuel 10:6 (ESV) Then the Spirit of the LORD will rush upon you, and you will prophesy with them and be turned into another man.

Saul was made King and presented before the people.

1 Samuel 10:24 (ESV) And Samuel said to all the people, "Do you see him whom the LORD has chosen? There is none like him among all the people." And all the people shouted, "Long live the king!"

Saul started well, but then he sinned. Saul's pride and impatience led him to offer unlawful sacrifices. The Prophet Samuel rebuked him for his foolish act.

1 Samuel 13:13 (ESV) And Samuel said to Saul, "You have done foolishly. You have not kept the command of the LORD your God, with which he commanded you. For then the LORD would have established your kingdom over Israel forever.

Samuel prophesied that the kingdom would be taken from Saul and given to a man after God's own heart.

1 Samuel 13:14 (ESV) But now your kingdom shall not continue. The LORD has sought out a man

after his own heart, and the LORD has commanded him to be prince over his people, because you have not kept what the LORD commanded you."

The Prophet Samuel rebuked King Saul for doing what is evil in the sight of God. At this point in the story, we can clearly see the progression of a backsliding heart in Saul. Because of his pride and disobedience, Saul did what was right in his own eyes. Samuel, the moral compass of Saul and Israel, was ready to speak the words of God over the King in the hope he would repent and do the Word and will of the Lord.

1 Samuel 15:17-19 (ESV) And Samuel said, "Though you are little in your own eyes, are you not the head of the tribes of Israel? The LORD anointed you king over Israel. 18 And the LORD sent you on a mission and said, 'Go, devote to destruction the sinners, the Amalekites, and fight against them until they are consumed.' 19 Why then did you not obey the voice of the LORD? Why did you pounce on the spoil and do what was evil in the sight of the LORD?"

Because Saul rejected the word of the Lord, God rejected him as King.

1 Samuel 15:23 (ESV) For rebellion is as the sin of divination, and presumption is as iniquity and idolatry. Because you have rejected the word of the LORD, he has also rejected you from being king."

1 Samuel 15:26 (ESV) And Samuel said to Saul, "I will not return with you. For you have rejected the word of the LORD, and the LORD has rejected you from being king over Israel."

King Saul feared the people more than he feared God.

1 Samuel 15:24 (ESV) Saul said to Samuel, "I have sinned, for I have transgressed the commandment of the LORD and your words, because I feared the people and obeyed their voice.

The Lord has chosen David to be the next King of Israel.

1 Samuel 16:1 (ESV) The LORD said to Samuel, "How long will you grieve over Saul, since I have rejected him from being king over Israel? Fill your horn with oil, and go. I will send you to Jesse the Bethlehemite, for I have provided for myself a king among his sons."

1 Samuel 16:13 (ESV) Then Samuel took the horn of oil and anointed him in the midst of his brothers. And the Spirit of the LORD rushed upon David from that day forward. And Samuel rose up and went to Ramah.

In 1 Samuel chapter 10, we saw how the Spirit of God fell on Saul. Here in chapters 16, 18, and 19, we read that the Spirit of God left Saul, and a harmful spirit came upon him that tormented him. A man once so anointed by God with the Holy Spirit is now rejected and filled with an unholy spirit.

1 Samuel 16:14-15 ESV Now the Spirit of the LORD departed from Saul, and a harmful spirit from the LORD tormented him. (15) And Saul's servants said to him, "Behold now, a harmful spirit from God is tormenting you.

1 Samuel 18:10-11 ESV The next day a harmful spirit from God rushed upon Saul, and he raved within his house while David was playing the lyre, as he did day by day. Saul had his spear in his hand. (11) And Saul hurled the spear, for he thought, "I will pin David to the wall." But David evaded him twice.

1 Samuel 19:9 ESV Then a harmful spirit from the LORD came upon Saul, as he sat in his house with his spear in his hand. And David was playing the lyre.

Questions For Chapter 12

1. Who vowed to give her son to the Lord to serve Him all his life?

2. Who anointed Saul as the King of Israel?

3. Why did Samuel rebuke Saul?

4. Why did God reject Saul as king?

5. What happened to Saul after the Spirit of the Lord departed from him?

Chapter 13
BIBLICAL EXAMPLES OF BELIEVERS INFLUENCED BY DEMONIC SPIRITS (NEW TESTAMENT)

We have established that casting out demons was a major part of the gospel ministry.

Matthew 10:1-4 ESV And he called to him his twelve disciples and gave them authority over unclean spirits, to cast them out, and to heal every disease and every affliction. (2) The names of the twelve apostles are these: first, Simon, who is called Peter, and Andrew his brother; James the son of Zebedee, and John his brother; (3) Philip and Bartholomew; Thomas and Matthew the tax collector; James the son of Alphaeus, and Thaddaeus; (4) Simon the Zealot, and Judas Iscariot, who betrayed him.

Matthew 10:8 ESV Heal the sick, raise the dead, cleanse lepers, cast out demons. You received without paying; give without pay.

Mark 16:17 ESV And these signs will accompany those who believe: in my name they will cast out demons; they will speak in new tongues;

Let's look at some of the New Testament examples of those who had demonic activity. All of these walked with Jesus for a period of time or came to Him in faith. The only exception would be the last example, "the adulterous man in the Corinth Church." We presume he was a believer because he was a member of the church and was invited to come back into the fellowship in 2 Corinthians after he repented of his sexual immorality.

Peter

Peter was influenced by demonic spirits. From Peter's mouth came a rebuke towards our Lord. Our Lord looked at Peter. However, He addressed Satan. This demonic presence had to be more than being influenced or oppressed.

> **Mark 8:32-33 ESV And he said this plainly. And Peter took him aside and began to rebuke him. (33) But turning and seeing his disciples, he rebuked Peter and said, "Get behind me, Satan! For you are not setting your mind on the things of God, but on the things of man."**

Some would say that the Lord just gave Peter a strong rebuke. This idea is not following the laws of textual interpretation. The Greek language used in Mark 8:33 for "Get behind me, Satan" is the same Greek language used in Matthew 4:10 for "Be gone, Satan." When the Lord looked at Peter and started speaking, it was as though Satan himself was standing in front of Him.

> **Matthew 4:10 ESV Then Jesus said to him, "Be gone, Satan! For it is written, "'You shall worship the Lord your God and him only shall you serve.'"**

Judas

Judas was influenced by the demonic. Judas always seems to catch a bad rap for his entire ministry time with Jesus. Criticizing the complete ministry of Judas should not be so. Our Lord chose him as one of the twelve disciples and sent him out to heal the sick and cast out demons. We know our Lord's teaching that a house cannot be divided against itself, so Satan can't cast out Satan. Judas was an active believing member of the faith until he opened the door of his heart, and the demonic was allowed to enter him.

> **Luke 22:3-4 ESV Then Satan entered into Judas called Iscariot, who was of the number of the twelve. (4) He went away and conferred with the chief priests and officers how he might betray him to them.**

Daughter Of Abraham

The "daughter of Abraham" was influenced by demonic spirits. Our Lord healed the "daughter of Abraham" by casting out a demon. Her father was not Abraham, but the term identified her as a devoted Jewish woman. Was she a believer in Jesus and therefore under the classification of having imputed righteousness? The Bible is silent concerning her spiritual status. Consequently, we cannot argue either way.

> **Luke 13:11-17 ESV And behold, there was a woman who had had a disabling spirit for eighteen years. She was bent over and could not fully straighten herself. (12) When Jesus saw her, he called her over and said to her, "Woman, you are freed from your disability." (13) And he laid his hands on her, and immediately she was**

made straight, and she glorified God. (14) But the ruler of the synagogue, indignant because Jesus had healed on the Sabbath, said to the people, "There are six days in which work ought to be done. Come on those days and be healed, and not on the Sabbath day." (15) Then the Lord answered him, "You hypocrites! Does not each of you on the Sabbath untie his ox or his donkey from the manger and lead it away to water it? (16) And ought not this woman, a daughter of Abraham whom Satan bound for eighteen years, be loosed from this bond on the Sabbath day?" (17) As he said these things, all his adversaries were put to shame, and all the people rejoiced at all the glorious things that were done by him.

Ananias And Sapphira

Ananias and Sapphira were influenced by demonic spirits. Was Ananias and Sapphira a part of the church? Again, we cannot speak from the position of silence. However, it would seem they were fulfilling the teaching of Acts 2, spoken by the Apostles.

Acts 2:42-47 (ESV) And they devoted themselves to the apostles' teaching and the fellowship, to the breaking of bread and the prayers. 43 And awe came upon every soul, and many wonders and signs were being done through the apostles. 44 And all who believed were together and had all things in common. 45 And they were selling their possessions and belongings and distributing the proceeds to all, as any had need. 46 And day by day, attending the temple together and breaking bread in their homes, they received their food with

glad and generous hearts, 47 praising God and having favor with all the people. And the Lord added to their number day by day those who were being saved.

In Acts 2:45, we see the early believers selling their possessions and sharing them with all the brothers. This benevolence is the first time we see this in action. In Acts 5:1, Ananias seemed to follow the Apostolic teaching of Acts 2:42-27. Therefore, from this, we can assume he and his wife were a part of the body of Christ. Again, this is just a strong assumption based on limited Scriptural knowledge. Those who jump on the premise that Ananias and Sapphira were just two lost religious people trying to earn favor are certainly taking a lot of liberty with the Word of God and speaking a lot amid Biblical silence. The name Ananias means "whom Jehovah has graciously given." All the commentaries I have researched claim that Ananias was a Christian in Jerusalem. Sapphira was the wife of Ananias. Sapphira is only mentioned by name in Acts 5:1. Her name means "sapphire."

Ananias and Sapphira did not have to sell their property, and they did not have to give the money to the Apostles. These things were their choices. The Scriptures suggest they were following the lead of the Apostle's teachings and the example of the other Christians. However, it says in Acts 5:3 that Satan had filled his heart to lie to the Holy Spirit. This sin resulted in the death of both Ananias and Sapphira. The Greek word for Satan is "Satanas" and means the accuser of the brethren himself. It is not referring to a lesser demonic spirit. The heart of Ananias is the soul of the inner man. This soul first includes the mind (the fountain and seat of thoughts, understanding, and intelligence). Secondly, it consists of the emotions (the fountain and seat of the passions, desires, appetites, and affections). Thirdly it includes the will (the fountain and seat of the actions, choices, purposes, and endeavors). Although we cannot argue from silence, the Scriptures suggest that Ananias and Sapphira were Christians in fellowship with a group of believers in Jerusalem who fell under demonic influence.

> **Acts 5:1-6 ESV But a man named Ananias, with his wife Sapphira, sold a piece of property, (2) and with his wife's knowledge he kept back for himself some of the proceeds and brought only a part of it and laid it at the apostles' feet. (3) But Peter said, "Ananias, why has Satan filled your heart to lie to the Holy Spirit and to keep back for yourself part of the proceeds of the land? (4) While it remained unsold, did it not remain your own? And after it was sold, was it not at your disposal? Why is it that you have contrived this deed in your heart? You have not lied to man but to God." (5) When Ananias heard these words, he fell down and breathed his last. And great fear came upon all who heard of it. (6) The young men rose and wrapped him up and carried him out and buried him.**

The Adulterous Man In Corinth Church Turned Over To Satan

The adulterous man in the Corinth church was influenced by demonic spirits. There was a man in the church who was guilty of sexual immorality. Paul told the Corinth believers to put him out of the church. They are told how to conduct the proper discipline. They are to excommunicate him from the fellowship. Secondly, they are to pray a certain way. In their prayers, they are to remove any physical protection so that his flesh falls under destruction and his spirit would be saved when he stood before the Lord in the day of the Lord. 1 Corinthians 5:1-5 is an interesting passage that could cause a lot of theological debates in some circles. Debating man's doctrinal or denominational stance is not the intent of this book. The main question would be enough to cause a discussion. Was this man a saved church member?

When reading just the 1 Corinthians 5:1-5 section, we would have to ask, why was he a part of the church if he was not saved? Why did Paul equate his actions to those of lost people if he was not saved? If he was not saved, why did Paul pronounce judgment? He had said in 1 Corinthians 5:12-13 that we judge only those within the fellowship and not those outside the faith. Therefore, based on solid biblical evidence, we can assume this man was a backslidden believer. We should not use the last part of 5:5 to make a rash statement that this proves he was a lost religious man unless we can Biblically answer the questions posed earlier.

Based on that assumption, we see in 1 Corinthians 5:5 that the body can be turned over to demonic influence to be buffeted for a season so that the person would repent of his sins.

1 Corinthians 5:1-5 ESV (1) It is actually reported that there is sexual immorality among you, and of a kind that is not tolerated even among pagans, for a man has his father's wife. (2) And you are arrogant! Ought you not rather to mourn? Let him who has done this be removed from among you. (3) For though absent in body, I am present in spirit; and as if present, I have already pronounced judgment on the one who did such a thing. (4) When you are assembled in the name

of the Lord Jesus and my spirit is present, with the power of our Lord Jesus, (5) you are to deliver this man to Satan for the destruction of the flesh, so that his spirit may be saved in the day of the Lord.

1 Corinthians 5:12-13 (ESV) For what have I to do with judging outsiders? Is it not those inside the church whom you are to judge? 13 God judges those outside. "Purge the evil person from among you."

Here in 2 Corinthians 2:6-11 we find the man guilty of sexual immorality in 1 Corinthians 5:1-5 repentant and restored within the body of Christ. Paul tells the man's church family to forgive him and restore him to the fellowship. This text seems to validate that the man was saved but backslidden in sexual sins.

2 Corinthians 2:6-11 ESV (6) For such a one, this punishment by the majority is enough, (7) so you should rather turn to forgive and comfort him, or he may be overwhelmed by excessive sorrow. (8) So I beg you to reaffirm your love for him. (9) For this is why I wrote, that I might test you and know whether you are obedient in everything. (10) Anyone whom you forgive, I also forgive. Indeed, what I have forgiven, if I have forgiven anything, has been for your sake in the presence of Christ, (11) so that we would not be outwitted by Satan; for we are not ignorant of his designs.

Questions For Chapter 13

1. According to Matthew 10:1-4, what authority did Jesus give his twelve disciples?

2. In Matthew 4:10, who did Jesus address as "Satan"?

3. Who was the "daughter of Abraham" mentioned in Luke 13:11-17, and what did Jesus do for her?

4. In Acts 5:1-6, why did Peter rebuke Ananias, and what was the consequence of his actions?

5. According to 1 Corinthians 5:1-5, what action did Paul instruct the Corinth church to take regarding a man guilty of sexual immorality?

Chapter 14
DELIVERANCE MINISTRY FOR ALL CHRISTIANS IS A MANDATE FROM GOD

Have you viewed the activity of "casting out demons" as being for a few spiritual warriors whom God called for such a ministry? Do you find yourself ignoring anything dealing with the arena of "spiritual warfare?" When you hear about "deliverance ministry," are your thoughts driven to some horror movie? Do you equate "deliverance ministry" as an activity only assigned to and performed by charismatic Christians?

Many over the years have made a name for themselves by having a deliverance ministry. Again, we can find ourselves departmentalizing the body of Christ. There is no special spiritual gift or office for spiritual warfare and deliverance ministry, just like there is no particular office or spiritual gift of intercession. Yet we will have a few in our services or ministries that we call our intercessors. All believers are called to intercession. All believers are called to the deliverance ministry.

Our Lord Jesus Christ regularly casts demons out of people. Many were healed physically, emotionally, and mentally by having a demon cast out.

Matthew 12:25-28 ESV Knowing their thoughts, he said to them, "Every kingdom divided against itself is laid waste, and no city or house divided against itself will stand. (26) And if Satan casts out Satan, he is divided against himself. How then will his kingdom stand? (27) And if I cast out demons by Beelzebul, by whom do your sons cast them out? Therefore they will be your judges. (28) But if it is by the Spirit of God that I cast out demons, then the kingdom of God has come upon you.

Our Lord taught that casting out demons is an act of faith, just like any other spiritual mandate we are called to do. Nothing is impossible for us if we have the faith of a mustard seed. It is not having a big faith in a little God. It is having an everyday faith in a big God. How big is your God in your eyes and mind?

Matthew 17:15-20 ESV said, "Lord, have mercy on my son, for he is an epileptic and he suffers terribly. For often he falls into the fire, and often into the water. (16) And I brought him to your disciples, and they could not heal him." (17) And Jesus answered, "O faithless and twisted generation, how long am I to be with you? How long am I to bear with you? Bring him here to me." (18) And Jesus rebuked the demon, and it came out of him, and the boy was healed instantly. (19) Then the disciples came to Jesus privately and said, "Why could we not cast it out?" (20) He said to them, "Because of your little faith. For truly, I say to you, if you have faith like a grain of mustard seed, you will say to this mountain, 'Move from here to there,' and it will move, and nothing will be impossible for you."

Mothers recognized that some sicknesses with their children were caused by demonic activity. When we come to Jesus by faith, the demons must flee.

> ***Mark 7:25-30 ESV** But immediately a woman whose little daughter had an unclean spirit heard of him and came and fell down at his feet. (26) Now the woman was a Gentile, a Syrophoenician by birth. And she begged him to cast the demon out of her daughter. (27) And he said to her, "Let the children be fed first, for it is not right to take the children's bread and throw it to the dogs." (28) But she answered him, "Yes, Lord; yet even the dogs under the table eat the children's crumbs." (29) And he said to her, "For this statement you may go your way; the demon has left your daughter." (30) And she went home and found the child lying in bed and the demon gone.*

> ***James 4:7 (ESV)** Submit yourselves therefore to God. Resist the devil, and he will flee from you.*

Deliverance ministry allows people to be free from the captivity of demonic oppression and control to be captured by the Lord Jesus Christ to do His will.

> ***2 Timothy 2:24-26 ESV** And the Lord's servant must not be quarrelsome but kind to everyone, able to teach, patiently enduring evil, (25) correcting his opponents with gentleness. God may perhaps grant them repentance leading to a knowledge of the truth, (26) and they may come to their senses and escape from the snare of the devil, after being captured by him to do his will.*

Questions For Chapter 14

1. Is the ministry of "casting out demons" limited to a select group of spiritual warriors chosen by God?

2. Do some people overlook or ignore the concept of "spiritual warfare"?

3. Is the term "deliverance ministry" often associated with horror movies?

4. Is "deliverance ministry" exclusively performed by charismatic Christians?

5. According to Jesus' teachings, is casting out demons an act of faith?

Chapter 15
THE ENEMY STANDS BEFORE GOD, READY TO ACCUSE US

The capabilities, power, and authority of the enemy are not infinite. He cannot operate outside the bounds of God's sovereignty. Satan always has and always will, until final judgment, report to the One who created him. God was, God is, and God will always be the King of Kings and have the last word. Our heavenly Father has no limitation in knowledge, presence, or power. He is in all places simultaneously (His Omnipresence) and knows everything happening (His Omniscient) in His created universe. He has all power (His Omnipotent) to do anything he chooses to do at any time.

As believers, we must realize we are armed and dangerous to the demonic forces of hell. How much do you understand concerning the power and operation of God versus Satan? Do you know the authority you possess as a child of the King?

The enemy, the devil, is unlike God. God created the angels. When one-third fell away and followed the devil, they still maintained the status of just being created spirits. Therefore, being created beings, they are limited in time, space, matter, authority, and power. The enemy and the demons are not all-knowing or all-powerful, nor can they be in more than one place at a time. This information is essential because, to hear Christians speak, one would think that Satan is likened to our God in that he can be all over the universe at the same time and is all-knowing and all-powerful. This thinking is simply untrue, unbiblical, and surely gives the enemy more right in and over our lives than he usually has the authority and power to do so.

The first step of a believer having a demon or being influenced by a demon is having an open door. We can open the door to the demonic through sins of commission (Doing what I know to be sin) or sins of omission (Not doing what I know to be good, moral, or neglecting daily Biblical disciplines). We saw in Chapter 3 Biblical examples of those who gave an open door to the demonic and the consequences of such.

The Bible states that Satan and his demonic host are liars and accusers. There are five ways the enemy accuses us.

1. He accuses us to God.
2. He accuses God to us.
3. He accuses us to others.
4. He accuses others to us.
5. He accuses us to us.

Let's look at Biblical examples of Satan's standing before God, accusing His saints. This accusation would be #1 on the list. "He accuses us to God." If we listen to these accusations, we have given the enemy an open door to influence and oppress us.

Questions For Chapter 15

1. Can the enemy operate outside the bounds of God's sovereignty? Why? Explain.

2. Does God possess unlimited knowledge, presence, and power?

3. What is the status of the fallen angels who followed the devil?

4. Is Satan all-knowing and all-powerful like God?

5. How can a believer open the door to the influence of demons?

Chapter 16
THE STORY OF JOB

Notice a couple of things from Job 1:6-12. Even though Satan has been cast out of heaven as his place of residence, according to Job 1:6, he still has access to come before God, his creator, to accuse mankind.

Job 1:6 ESV Now there was a day when the sons of God came to present themselves before the LORD, and Satan also came among them.

In Job 1:7, we see that the enemy must give God an account of his activities. Notice also in Job 1:7 that the enemy roams the earth seeking whom he may accuse and attack.

Job 1:7 ESV The LORD said to Satan, "From where have you come?" Satan answered the LORD and said, "From going to and fro on the earth, and from walking up and down on it."

Job 1:8 shows us that it was God who pointed out Job before the enemy by praising Job's faith and devotion.

Job 1:8 ESV And the LORD said to Satan, "Have you considered my servant Job, that there is none like him on the earth, a blameless and upright man, who fears God and turns away from evil?"

In Job 1:9, we see a couple of things. The first thing is that in the enemy's roaming the earth, Job certainly had caught his attention. The second thing is being who he is; the enemy could not help himself in casting an accusation against Job. Notice that in the charge, the enemy agreed with God that Job feared God.

> **Job 1:9 ESV Then Satan answered the LORD and said, "Does Job fear God for no reason?**

In Job 1:10, we see in the accusations of the enemy a revelation of the blessing of God upon Job. The enemy was testifying about how much God had blessed Job.

> **Job 1:10 ESV Have you not put a hedge around him and his house and all that he has, on every side? You have blessed the work of his hands, and his possessions have increased in the land.**

In Job 1:11, we find an interesting statement from the enemy. He pleaded for God to reach out His hand and touch Job's life and possessions. This revelation reveals that the devil could only do what God allowed and was limited in operation. Satan had tried to tempt God. However, God cannot be tempted, nor can He tempt anyone. Again, we see what the enemy does best. He cast another accusation against Job by saying that Job would curse God.

> **Job 1:11 ESV But stretch out your hand and touch all that he has, and he will curse you to your face."**

In Job 1:12, we see how God allowed something and why He did what He did. By God stretching out His hand, it means that He is pulling His hand of protection off and allowing the enemy the authority to touch the life of the person. God's hand of protection over Job, his family, and his possessions was pulled back. The devil was given the authority to go down and tempt Job. This affliction was done by taking that which was in God's hand and placing it in the enemy's hand. However, God never gives complete, unwatched control. He limited what the enemy could do to Job.

> **Job 1:6 ESV 12) And the LORD said to Satan, "Behold, all that he has is in your hand. Only against him do not stretch out your hand." So Satan went out from the presence of the LORD.**

Questions For Chapter 16

1. Does Satan still have access to come before God and accuse mankind?

2. What did God point out to Satan about Job in Job 1:8?

3. What revelation did the enemy make about God's blessings upon Job in Job 1:10?

4. What authority did God give to the enemy in Job 1:12?

5. Did God give the enemy complete, unwatched control over Job?

Chapter 17
THE STORY OF JOSHUA

Here in the Book of Zechariah, we will look at the access the enemy has to God the Father and the angels. Satan presented himself before God in heaven in Job 1:6, which we looked at earlier, but also here in Zechariah 3:1-7.

First, look at Zechariah 3:1. We are not sure if Satan was standing at the right hand of God or the right hand of Joshua, but we know that to stand or sit at the right hand is to stand or sit in a position of authority. It would seem from the language used that Satan was standing at the right hand of Joshua, believing he had a place of authority in his life and affairs.

> **Zechariah 3:1 ESV Then he showed me Joshua the high priest standing before the angel of the LORD, and Satan standing at his right hand to accuse him.**

The phrase "the angel of the Lord" is used throughout the Old Testament as a name for the pre-incarnate Lord Jesus Christ. It shows Joshua having an audience with the pre-incarnate Christ. It is an awesome thing to stand "before" the Lord. Satan, who is at the right hand of Joshua, is there to accuse him, which is what he does. Notice this, if you will. If Joshua is facing the Lord and the enemy is at Joshua's right hand, then the enemy is standing in a place of authority in Joshua's life and affairs. This positioning would mean the enemy stands at the Lord's left hand. Standing or sitting on the left hand is the lowliest position or place of having no authority. The enemy had no voice or position of authority over our Lord, nor did he have any authority over Joshua while they stood before the Lord.

In Zechariah 3:2, the Lord spoke out to Satan first. The word "rebuke" is an excellent word for an intensive Bible study. It carries strong authority and power. It shuts the mouths of God's enemies and releases His will and judgment. It would seem that Satan might have already cast out accusations earlier because the rebuke would be like the Lord saying, "Satan, shut your mouth!"

> ***Zechariah 3:2 ESV And the LORD said to Satan, "The LORD rebuke you, O Satan! The LORD who has chosen Jerusalem rebuke you! Is not this a brand plucked from the fire?"***

As the High Priest, Joshua was the spokesperson and the representative for the nation and the Holy City of Jerusalem. The Lord was about to establish Joshua before his enemy. The Lord also established the authority of His Holy City to rebuke their enemies. The Lord shows His love for Joshua and Jerusalem and that nothing can separate them from His love. The Apostle Paul gives a clear statement in Romans 8:33-39 concerning God's love toward us.

> ***Romans 8:33-39 ESV Who shall bring any charge against God's elect? It is God who justifies. (34) Who is to condemn? Christ Jesus is the one who died—more than that, who was raised—who is at the right hand of God, who indeed is interceding for us. (35) Who shall separate us from the love of Christ? Shall tribulation, or distress, or persecution, or famine, or nakedness, or danger,***

or sword? (36) As it is written, "For your sake we are being killed all the day long; we are regarded as sheep to be slaughtered." (37) No, in all these things we are more than conquerors through him who loved us. (38) For I am sure that neither death nor life, nor angels nor rulers, nor things present nor things to come, nor powers, (39) nor height nor depth, nor anything else in all creation, will be able to separate us from the love of God in Christ Jesus our Lord.

In Zechariah 3:3, we see that Joshua was clothed in filthy clothes. Joshua, the Priest, stood before the Lord as one polluted and unclean. He not only stands there representing his sins and brokenness, but his clothes represent Israel's sin, corruption, and brokenness. They were all unclean and separated from God. They only had their self-righteousness to trust in, which was as filthy rags.

Take notice that in all this activity and drama taking place, Joshua never spoke a word. This silence could have been due to the awe and fear he felt standing before God, the Lord Jesus Christ, the host of angels, and Satan. Joshua could be ashamed that as a High Priest, he was expected to maintain a high level of righteousness and holiness before God and man, and here he was, standing before the Lord in filthy rags. All we know for sure is that he spoke nothing. One thing to note though, is that he remained standing. This physical position is interesting to me. As the song "I Can Only Imagine" written by Bart Millard of "MercyMe says…

Surrounded by Your glory, what will my heart feel?
Will I dance for you Jesus, or in awe of you be still?
Will I stand in your presence, or to my knees will I fall?
Will I sing hallelujah? Will I be able to speak at all?

I can only imagine

Zechariah 3:3 ESV Now Joshua was standing before the angel, clothed with filthy garments.

By the law of Moses, the High Priest's garments were to be for glory and beauty. Therefore, they were of the best material and were to remain spotless. The garments were the physical items that set him apart for the priesthood.

Exodus 28:2-3 ESV And you shall make holy garments for Aaron your brother, for glory and for beauty. (3) You shall speak to all the skillful, whom I have filled with a spirit of skill, that they make Aaron's garments to consecrate him for my priesthood.

Joshua did not have clean linen to minister and do the duty of his office as a High Priest. But Joshua's garments were a shame and reproach to him and his office of priesthood. However, in those dirty, filthy garments, he found himself standing before the Lord. I think that it could go without saying, but I will mention that the filthy garments represent the condition of our souls outside Christ before we were washed in the blood of the Lamb.

In Zechariah, we have some clue as to what might be going on within Joshua. The angel of the Lord commanded the other angels standing around. Joshua's filthy garments were to be removed from him. For a period of time, Joshua stood naked before the Lord and the angels of heaven. I believe this is the condition we all will be in one day as we stand before the judgment seat of Christ. We stand there naked with nothing but being robed in the righteousness of Christ. This nakedness was the condition of the Laodicea church, yet she failed to realize it. They felt they were robed in their self-righteousness.

> **Zechariah 3:4 ESV And the angel said to those who were standing before him, "Remove the filthy garments from him." And to him he said, "Behold, I have taken your iniquity away from you, and I will clothe you with pure vestments."**

> **Revelation 3:16-17 ESV So, because you are lukewarm, and neither hot nor cold, I will spit you out of my mouth. (17) For you say, I am rich, I have prospered, and I need nothing, not realizing that you are wretched, pitiable, poor, blind, and naked.**

How can I assume to know what Joshua might have been thinking? In Zechariah 3:2, the Lord addressed Satan. At the beginning of Zechariah 3:4, the Lord addressed the angels around Him. Finally, in the latter part of Zechariah 3:4, the Lord addresses Joshua. Have you ever had someone address you in answering a look of surprise, puzzlement, or confusion on your face? Whether the Lord knew what Joshua was thinking or saw the countenance on his face is unclear, but something prompted the Lord to tell Joshua what He had done for the priest. All the sin within the heart of Joshua was taken away at the spoken word of our Lord. The secret places of the heart that no one knew about except Joshua and God Himself had now been laid open and made pure. Joshua must have been overwhelmed when he heard the words "I will clothe you with pure vestments."

Joshua's garments did not get in the filthy position by Joshua and the people walking in holiness and righteousness. There was a lifestyle of sin and disobedience.

Satan had been given an open door through temptation. Now we see the results of Joshua, the High Priest allowing sin to take him further than he wanted to go, costing him more than he wanted to pay, and keeping him longer than he wanted to stay. Life is a lot like a chess match. We move, and the enemy moves. We move again, which the enemy quickly countermoves. This chess match continues until we find ourselves being checkmated by the enemy. In these situations, we may feel we have lost the chess game of life because the enemy holds us in checkmate, and we have nowhere else to go. Praise be to God that our Lord scans the board of life and declares to us, "Lift up your heads, shake off the dirt, and rejoice because there is still one move to make." What seems to be a checkmate move by Satan is an opportunity for God to declare that He has one more action, and it will checkmate the enemy.

Joshua was filthy in the sins and condemnation of the nation and the priesthood. There seemed to be no way out. He seemed checkmated. Now he stood before the counsel of heaven with his accuser and enemy at his right-hand side. The Lord God of heaven makes his move. Joshua's sins had been taken away. He was about to be clothed with new garments. Amen! Knowing that Satan was standing there watching and hearing all this makes the Scripture in Colossians 2:13-15 mean more. I believe this event in Zechariah 3 was the Old Testament shadow of the New Testament substance.

> ***Colossians 2:13-15 ESV And you, who were dead in your trespasses and the uncircumcision of your flesh, God made alive together with him, having forgiven us all our trespasses, (14) by canceling the record of debt that stood against us with its legal demands. This he set aside, nailing it***

to the cross. (15) He disarmed the rulers and authorities and put them to open shame, by triumphing over them in him.

The provision was made for Joshua's cleansing. Christ gave orders to the angels that stood around in the counsel of heaven. I am sure it was a great pleasure for the angels to see Joshua positioned in a better state. It would be amiss if I did not state that our Lord hated the stained, polluted, corrupted rags that Joshua wore, knowing that they represented a condition of the heart. Yet, our Lord did not chide him or push him away. This event is a real picture of God's love and grace in action. Notice the authority with which the Lord spoke in Zechariah 3:4.

Zechariah 3:4 ESV "Behold, I have taken your iniquity away from you, and I will clothe you with pure vestments."

Matthew 7:28-29 ESV And when Jesus finished these sayings, the crowds were astonished at his teaching, (29) for he was teaching them as one who had authority, and not as their scribes.

Our Lord had the authority to forgive sins in heaven long before He exercised that authority on earth.

Matthew 9:2-8 ESV And behold, some people brought to him a paralytic, lying on a bed. And when Jesus saw their faith, he said to the paralytic, "Take heart, my son; your sins are forgiven." (3) And behold, some of the scribes said to themselves, "This man is blaspheming." (4) But Jesus, knowing their thoughts, said, "Why do you think evil in your hearts? (5) For which is

easier, to say, 'Your sins are forgiven,' or to say, 'Rise and walk'? (6) But that you may know that the Son of Man has authority on earth to forgive sins"—he then said to the paralytic—"Rise, pick up your bed and go home." (7) And he rose and went home. (8) When the crowds saw it, they were afraid, and they glorified God, who had given such authority to men.

Matthew 28:18 ESV And Jesus came and said to them, "All authority in heaven and on earth has been given to me.

When God forgives our sins, he causes our iniquity to pass from us so that it might not appear anymore against us to condemn us. Joshua was putting off the old man and was about to put on the new man. Joshua not only had the shame of his filthiness removed, but the shame of his nakedness was covered.

Ephesians 4:20-24 ESV But that is not the way you learned Christ!— (21) assuming that you have heard about him and were taught in him, as the truth is in Jesus, (22) to put off your old self, which belongs to your former manner of life and is corrupt through deceitful desires, (23) and to be renewed in the spirit of your minds, (24) and to put on the new self, created after the likeness of God in true righteousness and holiness.

What joy the Lord must have felt as he watched the transformation of Joshua. His filthy rags and sins had been removed, and now in Zechariah 3:5, we see that he was being clothed with new garments. And in all of this, the Lord Jesus Christ stood by watching.

> ***Zechariah 3:5 ESV And I said, "Let them put a clean turban on his head." So they put a clean turban on his head and clothed him with garments. And the angel of the LORD was standing by.***

> ***Zechariah 3:6-7 ESV And the angel of the LORD solemnly assured Joshua, (7) "Thus says the LORD of hosts: If you will walk in my ways and keep my charge, then you shall rule my house and have charge of my courts, and I will give you the right of access among those who are standing here.***

I want to share something from this passage that ought to really excite you. It deals with "the Right of Passage." We see in Zechariah 3:6-7 that with the change of garments and the change of heart, the Lord gave Joshua a change of mission and authority. The Lord made a lot of "if-then" statements in the Word of God. One of the most popular is 2 Chronicles 7:14.

> ***2 Chronicles 7:14 ESV if my people who are called by my name humble themselves, and pray and seek my face and turn from their wicked ways, then I will hear from heaven and will forgive their sin and heal their land.***

In the "if-then" passages, we have God's promises if we do something. If we obey, then God will do something. The Lord told Joshua that **IF** he walked in the ways of God and kept His commandments, **THEN** Joshua would rule God's house and have the right to access His presence.

I want to speak about the right of access called "the Right of Passage." We should know what that means in the natural. Remember when your heart desired to be 13 and be called a teenager? Remember when you wanted to turn old enough to get your driver's license? These are just two examples of having the right of passage. It means we have moved into an area we had not traveled before.

> *Joshua 3:4 ESV Yet there shall be a distance between you and it, about 2,000 cubits in length. Do not come near it, in order that you may know the way you shall go, for you have not passed this way before."*

The Lord told Joshua that if he did what the Lord had commanded, he would have access or right of passage among all those standing among them. Think about it. This right of passage means that Joshua was given access to God the Father, the Son, the Angels, and the enemy's camp. Wow! As we read the New Testament, we find we have the same right and authority as believers. Now, this ought to add some new insight into spiritual warfare.

Remember what I have shared about how defeated Satan is? The Lord Jesus Christ went into hell and took the keys of death and the grave from the enemy. Then our Lord gave those keys to us. Satan is so defeated that he doesn't even have the keys to his own house. Glory! Therefore, if the enemy doesn't own the keys to his house, don't invite him to sit at your table.

Questions For Chapter 17

1. Who was standing at the right hand of Joshua in Zechariah 3:1?

2. What does the phrase "the angel of the Lord" represent in the Old Testament?

3. Why did Joshua remain silent while standing before the Lord in filthy garments?

4. What did the Lord declare to Joshua in Zechariah 3:4?

5. What condition was Joshua in before his transformation in Zechariah 3?

Chapter 18
THE STORY OF AHAB

Notice in 1 Kings 22:19-21 that a spirit came forward. This spirit was not from the heavenly host that stands on the right or left hand of the Lord because those are pure and holy angels who cannot lie or deceive. This outspoken voice approaching the Lord God of heaven had to come from an evil spirit. It could have been the devil, the father of lies, or it could have been just a lying spirit.

The evil lying spirit said that he would entice or prevail upon Ahab. Evil spirits love to harm men, which is why they go about seeking whom they may devour.

> *1 Kings 22:19-21 ESV   And Micaiah said, "Therefore hear the word of the LORD: I saw the LORD sitting on his throne, and all the host of heaven standing beside him on his right hand and on his left; (20) and the LORD said, 'Who will entice Ahab, that he may go up and fall at Ramoth-gilead?' And one said one thing, and another said another. (21) Then a spirit came forward and stood before the LORD, saying, 'I will entice him.'*

Notice that in 1 Kings 22:22, the Lord asked the evil spirit how he would entice Ahab. What way and method did he propose to persuade Ahab to go up to Ramoth? From the surface, it would seem God our Father, the Creator of all, is introduced in this narrative as asking a question in order to gain information. However, it is essential to see that God is not ignorant of the schemes of the evil spirit. This question was God's way of bringing the scheme out in the open and showing everyone that, as God, He controlled what was happening. The evil spirit was going to place a lying spirit in the mouth of the prophets, which would provoke the prophets to encourage Ahab to go up in battle. The lying prophets would promise him success, as he had in former battles with the king of Syria. The lying mouths of the prophets encouraged Ahab with the prediction and caused him to believe it to be true. God knew that this would bring righteous judgment upon Ahab. Ahab's heart was already pronged to believe a lie over the truth, so it would be in his heart to receive the false words of the deceitful prophets. This deceitful heart sounds a lot like the church today. People with a heart prong to believe lies over truth have been given prophets whose mouths have been filled with lies for fame and profit.

> *1 Kings 22:22 And the LORD said to him, 'By what means?' And he said, 'I will go out, and will be a lying spirit in the mouth of all his prophets.' And he said, 'You are to entice him, and you shall succeed; go out and do so.'*

> *John 13:27-30 ESV Then after he had taken the morsel, Satan entered into him. Jesus said to him, "What you are going to do, do quickly." (28) Now no one at the table knew why he said this to him. (29) Some thought that, because Judas had the moneybag, Jesus was telling him, "Buy what we need for the feast," or that he should give something to the poor. (30) So, after receiving*

the morsel of bread, he immediately went out. And it was night.

In 1 Kings 22:23, we see the statement that the Lord placed a lying spirit in the mouth of the prophets. Again, this means that the Lord drew back His hand and allowed the lying spirit who stood before Him to go and do what he had suggested. The Lord will and has sent a strong delusion to make people believe that lie. The strong delusion will affect those whose minds were already predisposed to flatter Ahab. God continued the process that their heart had already headed towards.

> **1 Kings 22:23 Now therefore behold, the LORD has put a lying spirit in the mouth of all these your prophets; the LORD has declared disaster for you."**

> **2 Thessalonians 2:9-12 ESV (9) The coming of the lawless one is by the activity of Satan with all power and false signs and wonders, (10) and with all wicked deception for those who are perishing, because they refused to love the truth and so be saved. (11) Therefore God sends them a strong delusion, so that they may believe what is false, (12) in order that all may be condemned who did not believe the truth but had pleasure in unrighteousness.**

There it is. In chapter 16 we read about how the demonic attacked and influenced Job because the enemy wanted to show the world that Job was not a righteous man like God had claimed. The enemy wanted to show that Job loved and worshipped God because of his abundant blessings. The enemy was proven wrong on all accounts.

This outcome does not mean that Job was sinless. In Job 3:25, the righteous man speaks about his fears. This example shows us that the enemy seeks and desires to destroy certain people of faith, hoping they will turn against God.

Job 3:25 (ESV) For the thing that I fear comes upon me, and what I dread befalls me.

In chapter 17 we read about how Joshua and the nation had sinned. As the priest stood before the Lord, his priestly garments were nothing more than tattered, filthy rags. The enemy had his way in the nation and the priesthood. Now he stood before God the Son, the heavenly Father, the angels, and Joshua, most likely proud of his achievements. However, the enemy did not take into account the mercy and grace of a loving Savior who forgave Joshua and dressed him in new priestly garments. In modern Christianity, we call this deliverance and revival.

What man and the enemy meant for evil, God turned around and meant for good. This example shows us that we can also look like Joshua's dirty priestly garments because of sin, disobedience, and demonic influence. Satan will stand by to gloat on the successes of showing the Lord just how far we have fallen. However, we serve a risen Savior who does more than save people from their sinful nature. He is also in the restoration business of taking one of His children that found himself in need of returning to the Father. When one realizes his sin and disobedience have led him into a pigpen, the Father waits for him to return home to present him with a kingly robe, a ring, and new sandals.

Here in chapter 18, we see that Ahab seemed to surround himself with people who were demonized. Everything written about Ahab and his actions reveals his demonic oppression. Likewise, in the New Testament, Jesus told the religious Pharisees that their father was Satan, and they fulfilled his deeds.

> ***John 8:39-44 (ESV) They answered him, "Abraham is our father." Jesus said to them, "If you were Abraham's children, you would be doing the works Abraham did, 40 but now you seek to kill me, a man who has told you the truth that I heard from God. This is not what Abraham did. 41 You are doing the works your father did." They said to him, "We were not born of sexual immorality. We have one Father—even God." 42 Jesus said to them, "If God were your Father, you would love me, for I came from God and I am here. I came not of my own accord, but he sent me. 43 Why do you not understand what I say? It is because you cannot bear to hear my word. 44 You are of your father the devil, and your will is to do your father's desires. He was a murderer from the beginning, and does not stand in the truth, because there is no truth in him. When he lies, he speaks out of his own character, for he is a liar and the father of lies.***

Questions For Chapter 18

1. Who was the spirit that came forward in 1 Kings 22:19-21, and what did he propose to do?

2. In 1 Kings 22:22, what did the Lord ask the evil spirit, and how did the evil spirit respond?

3. In John 13:27-30, who entered Judas, and what did Jesus say to him?

4. What did God do in 1 Kings 22:23 regarding the lying spirit and the prophets?

5. According to 2 Thessalonians 2:9-12, why does God send a strong delusion, and who does it affect?

Chapter 19
WHAT THE DEVIL CAN AND CANNOT DO:
THE ENEMY'S LIMITATIONS

I t is vital to know what the devil and the demons can and cannot do to us before we run off doing spiritual warfare. Suppose you were a boxer. You would train for your next bout to ensure you have the stamina to maintain fifteen rounds. Along with the training, you would study your opponent to know how he moves and counters with your actions. You certainly would want to learn your opponent's strengths and weaknesses. The same is true in spiritual warfare. We do not wish to honor or praise Satan and his demonic forces in any way, nor do we want to devote all our time to the demonic that we become out of balance.

We certainly want to know every way that Satan and his demons are able to affect us. We are commanded to know his schemes. To keep us from fruitless activity by doing things unnecessarily, it might also be helpful to know some things the enemy cannot do. The enemy has been given great freedom to work among the world of mankind during this phase of history. The fact that he is roaming about seeking whom he may devour tells me that he has the right to create chaos in the lives of many.

1 Peter 5:8 (ESV) Be sober-minded; be watchful. Your adversary the devil prowls around like a roaring lion, seeking someone to devour.

Before looking at what the enemy can and cannot do, let's look at some of the Father's commands and warnings he gave concerning our war against the demonic forces of darkness. The Apostle Paul tells us in Ephesians 2:1-3 that it is only natural for spiritually lost people to follow Satan and do his deeds.

> **Ephesians 2:1-3 ESV And you were dead in the trespasses and sins (2) in which you once walked, following the course of this world, following the prince of the power of the air, the spirit that is now at work in the sons of disobedience— (3) among whom we all once lived in the passions of our flesh, carrying out the desires of the body and the mind, and were by nature children of wrath, like the rest of mankind.**

> **John 12:31 ESV Now is the judgment of this world; now will the ruler of this world be cast out.**

In 2 Corinthians 4:3-4, the Apostle Paul gives us great insight into the condition of spiritually lost people. Before I was saved, I had no idea the gospel message was veiled from me. I could not see the truth of God's love and the redemption He offered through His Son, our Lord Jesus Christ. Satan and his demonic host had blinded my mind hoping to keep me from seeing the light of the gospel and the glory of our Lord. Praise be to God, who wooed my heart with His Spirit until the day I cried out to Jesus to save me. And save me, He did.

> **2 Corinthians 4:3-4 ESV (3) And even if our gospel is veiled, it is veiled to those who are**

95

perishing. (4) In their case the god of this world has blinded the minds of the unbelievers, to keep them from seeing the light of the gospel of the glory of Christ, who is the image of God.

Paul teaches great lessons concerning spiritual warfare in Ephesians chapter 6. In 6:11-12, he tells us to put on our armor. This robing in armor is something we do and believe in by faith. Why do we need to do this, Paul? He tells us why we need to put on the armor. He says, "So that you may be able to stand against the schemes of the devil."

Then Paul tells us who we are fighting against. No, it is not against the church across the road and down the street. And pastors, we are not fighting against outspoken contentious church members that seem like our thorns in the flesh. They feel like thorns sometimes, and the temptation arises to wish and bless another church with their presence. Paul tells us our fight is against the demonic and lists them in rank like a military command from foot soldiers to the territorial generals.

Ephesians 6:11-12 ESV Put on the whole armor of God, that you may be able to stand against the schemes of the devil. (12) For we do not wrestle against flesh and blood, but against the rulers, against the authorities, against the cosmic powers over this present darkness, against the spiritual forces of evil in the heavenly places.

Paul repeats in Ephesians 6:13 the command concerning the armor in Ephesians 6:11. In verse 11, Paul instructs us to "put on the armor," but in 6:13, he tells us to "take up the armor." Again, it is what we do and believe by faith.

In Ephesians 6:11, Paul explains why by stating, "that you may be able to stand against the schemes of the devil." In 6:13, he says, "that you may be able to withstand in the evil day." We will face evil demonic forces in evil demonic times. We cannot give what we do not have. We cannot take up and put on what we do not possess.

An example is Ephesians 6:17 when Paul tells us to "take the helmet of salvation, and the sword of the Spirit, which is the word of God." This command is not just about owning or carrying a Bible. We must read and study the Word of God if we plan on using it as armor against the enemy.

> ***Ephesians 6:13-18 (ESV) Therefore take up the whole armor of God, that you may be able to withstand in the evil day, and having done all, to stand firm. 14 Stand therefore, having fastened on the belt of truth, and having put on the breastplate of righteousness, 15 and, as shoes for your feet, having put on the readiness given by the gospel of peace. 16 In all circumstances take up the shield of faith, with which you can extinguish all the flaming darts of the evil one; 17 and take the helmet of salvation, and the sword of the Spirit, which is the word of God, 18 praying at all times in the Spirit, with all prayer and supplication. To that end, keep alert with all perseverance, making supplication for all the saints,***

We can know a true believer from a false one who claims to be a Christian by their lifestyle. The fruit reveals the root. Every Christian will sin and even dwell in sin for a season. However, an authentic Christian cannot live in a lifestyle of sin. Our Lord Jesus Christ came to destroy the works of the enemy.

> ***1 John 3:8 ESV Whoever makes a practice of sinning is of the devil, for the devil has been sinning from the beginning. The reason the Son of God appeared was to destroy the works of the devil.***

Our Lord Jesus Christ knew He had to fulfill the reason He came for the redemption of mankind. He knew He would die as first prophesied in Genesis 3:15. In His arrest, scourging, and death on a cruel cross; Jesus wanted it to be understood that Satan was not empowered to do anything in His life. He could not cause it or stop it. Our Lord gave His life at the exact time He was supposed to, and no military, religious, or demonic group could change the events. God had spoken, and it was being fulfilled, right up to the words "It Is Finished."

> ***John 14:30-31 ESV I will no longer talk much with you, for the ruler of this world is coming. He has no claim on me, 31 but I do as the Father has commanded me, so that the world may know that I love the Father. Rise, let us go from here.***

Questions For Chapter 19

1. What is the significance of studying the opponent's strengths and weaknesses in spiritual warfare?

2. What is the role of Satan and his demonic forces in the lives of spiritually lost people?

3. How does Satan blind the minds of unbelievers?

4. Who are believers instructed to fight against in spiritual warfare?

5. What is the purpose of putting on the whole armor of God in spiritual warfare?

Chapter 20
THE ENEMY CAN NOT TOUCH THE "NEW SELF" BEGOTTEN BY GOD

When saved, we are spiritually born anew as children of a Holy God. From that point on, we carry within ourselves the human seed of our earthly parent and God's imperishable, holy seed.

1 Peter 1:22-23 (ESV) Having purified your souls by your obedience to the truth for a sincere brotherly love, love one another earnestly from a pure heart, 23 since you have been born again, not of perishable seed but of imperishable, through the living and abiding word of God;

Since our old Adamic nature was crucified in Christ, the seed of Christ within us gives rise to our new nature, which is replicated in the righteousness and holiness of our heavenly Father.

2 Corinthians 5:17 (ESV) Therefore, if anyone is in Christ, he is a new creation. The old has passed away; behold, the new has come.

Ephesians 4:22-24 (ESV) to put off your old self, which belongs to your former manner of life and is corrupt through deceitful desires, 23 and to be renewed in the spirit of your minds, 24 and to put on the new self, created after the likeness of God in true righteousness and holiness.

His holy seed creates within our spirit man a holy life, and just as the demonic cannot touch our holy God, he cannot touch our "new self." The Holy Spirit dwells in our spirit-man. Theologians debate whether this part can sin or not. Since the Holy Spirit dwells in my spirit, it is like the Holy of Holies, righteous and pure, as our heavenly Father is Holy.

The parts of a Christian the demonic can affect is the soulish man, which is the thoughts (the mind), the emotions (the feelings), and the will (our choices). He can also affect our physical body. These are areas in which the demonic gained dominion due to Adam and Eve's sin. When we were lost, we were children of the enemy and called children of wrath. Before salvation, when we were spiritually dead, the enemy stamped his rebellious and deceitful nature on us as his children.

>*Jeremiah 17:9-10 (ESV) The heart is deceitful above all things, and desperately sick; who can understand it? 10 "I the LORD search the heart and test the mind, to give every man according to his ways, according to the fruit of his deeds."*

>*Romans 6:15-18 (ESV) What then? Are we to sin because we are not under law but under grace? By no means! 16 Do you not know that if you present yourselves to anyone as obedient slaves, you are slaves of the one whom you obey, either of sin, which leads to death, or of obedience, which leads to righteousness? 17 But thanks be to God, that you who were once slaves of sin have become obedient from the heart to the standard of teaching to which you were committed, 18 and,*

having been set free from sin, have become slaves of righteousness.

Colossians 1:13-14 (ESV) He has delivered us from the domain of darkness and transferred us to the kingdom of his beloved Son, 14 in whom we have redemption, the forgiveness of sins.

Once saved, although the Adamic nature was crucified and our spirit man was quickened with the life of Christ, our physical bodies and souls continue to fight against God, His Word, and the leadership of His Spirit. As believers, we still battle daily concerning who we will follow. Will we obey God and His Word, or will we follow the desires of our flesh, the world, and the enemy?

Romans 7:14-20 (ESV) For we know that the law is spiritual, but I am of the flesh, sold under sin. 15 For I do not understand my own actions. For I do not do what I want, but I do the very thing I hate. 16 Now if I do what I do not want, I agree with the law, that it is good. 17 So now it is no longer I who do it, but sin that dwells within me. 18 For I know that nothing good dwells in me, that is, in my flesh. For I have the desire to do what is right, but not the ability to carry it out. 19 For I do not do the good I want, but the evil I do not want is what I keep on doing. 20 Now if I do what I do not want, it is no longer I who do it, but sin that dwells within me.

Romans 7:22-25 (ESV) For I delight in the law of God, in my inner being, 23 but I see in my members another law waging war against the law of my mind and making me captive to the law of sin that dwells in my members. 24 Wretched man that I am! Who will deliver me from this body of death? 25 Thanks be to God through Jesus Christ our Lord! So then, I myself serve the law of God with my mind, but with my flesh I serve the law of sin.

The Apostle Paul tells us in Romans 8:5-8 that a life lived in the flesh cannot please the Father. This outcome of displeasure is why we are commanded to walk in the Spirit. If we are commanded to walk in the Spirit, then we know it is possible to walk in the flesh. To walk in the Spirit is walking in faith, as it says in Hebrews 11:6.

Romans 8:5-8 (ESV) For those who live according to the flesh set their minds on the things of the flesh, but those who live according to the Spirit set their minds on the things of the Spirit. 6 For to set the mind on the flesh is death, but to set the mind on the Spirit is life and peace. 7 For the mind that is set on the flesh is hostile to God, for it does not submit to God's law; indeed, it cannot. 8 Those who are in the flesh cannot please God.

Paul instructs us in Romans 8:10-13 that we don't owe our flesh anything. We hear commercial after commercial that we deserve something and must demand to have it our way. These ads go against the teachings of God's Word, which tells me I deserve nothing but to die. I am dead in Christ, and my only life is in Christ. To follow the flesh is death, but there is life to be found in the Spirit.

Romans 8:10-13 (ESV) But if Christ is in you, although the body is dead because of sin, the Spirit is life because of righteousness. 11 If the

Spirit of him who raised Jesus from the dead dwells in you, he who raised Christ Jesus from the dead will also give life to your mortal bodies through his Spirit who dwells in you. 12 So then, brothers, we are debtors, not to the flesh, to live according to the flesh. 13 For if you live according to the flesh you will die, but if by the Spirit you put to death the deeds of the body, you will live.

Galatians 5:16-17 (ESV) But I say, walk by the Spirit, and you will not gratify the desires of the flesh. 17 For the desires of the flesh are against the Spirit, and the desires of the Spirit are against the flesh, for these are opposed to each other, to keep you from doing the things you want to do.

One of the critical elements of Ephesians 4:17-24 is the teaching received. The Apostle Paul says, "Assuming that you heard about Him and were taught in Him. Pastors who dare to teach the truth are vital in our walk with the Lord.

Ephesians 4:17-24 (ESV) Now this I say and testify in the Lord, that you must no longer walk as the Gentiles do, in the futility of their minds. 18 They are darkened in their understanding, alienated from the life of God because of the ignorance that is in them, due to their hardness of heart. 19 They have become callous and have given themselves up to sensuality, greedy to practice every kind of impurity. 20 But that is not the way you learned Christ!— 21 assuming that you have heard about Him and were taught in him, as the truth is in Jesus, 22 to put off your old self, which belongs to your former manner of life and is corrupt through deceitful desires, 23 and to be renewed in the spirit of your minds, 24 and to put on the new

self, created after the likeness of God in true righteousness and holiness.

We have established who we are in Christ and who He is in us. It should be a great source of comfort to you, knowing the enemy cannot access your spirit-man where the Holy Spirit dwells.

Questions For Chapter 20

1. What does it mean to be born anew as children of a Holy God?

2. How does the seed of Christ within us give rise to our new nature?

3. Which parts of a Christian can the demonic affect?

4. What does it mean to walk in the Spirit, and why is it important?

5. How does teaching affect a believer's walk with the Lord?

Chapter 21
THE ENEMY CAN NOT MAKE A PERSON SIN

The enemy can lead us to sinful waters but cannot make us drink. He can even "salt the oats" to make us crave that sinful water, but we are still responsible for any immoral acts we choose to engage in. Every temptation the enemy brings into our lives first starts with lust within our hearts. God has faithfully provided a way to escape every temptation the enemy brings into our lives.

> *James 1:13-15 (ESV) Let no one say when he is tempted, "I am being tempted by God," for God cannot be tempted with evil, and he himself tempts no one. 14 But each person is tempted when he is lured and enticed by his own desire. 15 Then desire when it has conceived gives birth to sin, and sin when it is fully grown brings forth death.*

> *1 Corinthians 10:13 (ESV) No temptation has overtaken you that is not common to man. God is faithful, and he will not let you be tempted beyond your ability, but with the temptation he will also provide the way of escape, that you may be able to endure it.*

There are some who, at times, feel it wise to blame God for what they are going through. If we need reminding, let me say again, "God cannot be tempted, nor will He tempt us." Therefore, if you are in the battle of temptation and seem to be under your circumstances, they are bottom-line issues of the heart being exposed. Remember, all temptation starts with the lust that resides in the heart. It is always in the plans of the Father to give us hope and what we need for a blessed future.

> ***Jeremiah 29:11 (ESV) For I know the plans I have for you, declares the LORD, plans for welfare and not for evil, to give you a future and a hope.***

Questions For Chapter 21

1. Can the enemy make us engage in immoral acts?

2. What role does lust play in the process of temptation?

3. Does God tempt people with evil?

4. How does God help us in the face of temptation?

5. What are the plans of the Father for our lives?

Chapter 22
THE ENEMY CAN NOT OVERPOWER A PERSON'S FREE WILL

Our free will is an irrevocable gift from God. Unless a person has willfully chosen to enter a covenant relationship with Satan or another pagan deity, these evil cosmic beings cannot automatically execute their will in a person's life. They can only do so when the person voluntarily relinquishes control to them. A person may have been given legal grounds or generational inheritances that allow demonic beings to be connected to them. However, we believe strongly the demonic cannot act out in a person's life without permission being granted by the person. This permission is usually done through acts of sin, such as intense anger or unforgiveness.

I listed a few Scriptural references on our free will so that we understand that the Christian life is a life of faith and choices. Paul tells us in Galatians 5:13 that we should not use our Christian freedom in Christ as an opportunity to sin or live worldly. Peter repeats this teaching in 1 Peter 2:16.

Galatians 5:13 (ESV) For you were called to freedom, brothers. Only do not use your freedom as an opportunity for the flesh, but through love serve one another.

1 Peter 2:16 (ESV) Live as people who are free, not using your freedom as a cover-up for evil, but living as servants of God.

Giving to the work of the ministry should not be done through guilt-ridden sermons leaving the impression that we MUST support a person or ministry. According to Philemon 1:14, our giving should be mandated by the leadership of the Holy Spirit upon the person's will.

> **Philemon 1:14 (ESV) but I preferred to do nothing without your consent in order that your goodness might not be by compulsion but of your own accord.**

Our walk should be in the Spirit and not in the flesh. James 2:12 tells us we will still be judged, not under the Law, but under the freedom of God's grace.

> **James 2:12 (ESV) So speak and so act as those who are to be judged under the law of liberty.**

Paul warns us in Galatians 5:1 that we are to walk in the spiritual freedom our Lord Jesus Christ gave us but not allow ourselves to be placed back under the yoke of the Law and sin.

> **Galatians 5:1 (ESV) For freedom Christ has set us free; stand firm therefore, and do not submit again to a yoke of slavery.**

John records the words of our Lord Jesus Christ in Revelation 3:20, as He addressed the church at Laodicea. Jesus is standing outside the church, knocking, as they are having their religious services. He is requesting to come in and join them in fellowship. It is the church's will or choice to invite Jesus in or not.

Revelation 3:20 (ESV) Behold, I stand at the door and knock. If anyone hears my voice and opens the door, I will come in to him and eat with him, and he with me.

The Apostle Paul instructs us that with every temptation, there is a way of escape, and that way is making the right choices in our Lord Jesus Christ. He tells us in 1 Corinthians 10:13 that temptation is common to all men, and we will not be tempted beyond our ability to choose.

1 Corinthians 10:13 (ESV) No temptation has overtaken you that is not common to man. God is faithful, and he will not let you be tempted beyond your ability, but with the temptation he will also provide the way of escape, that you may be able to endure it.

Questions For Chapter 22

1. Can evil demonic beings execute their will in a person's life without permission?

2. How can demonic beings be connected to a person's life?

3. What is the purpose of Christian freedom according to Galatians 5:13?

4. How should giving to the work of the ministry be approached?

5. How should believers walk in their freedom according to James 2:12?

Chapter 23
THE ENEMY CAN NOT ASSAULT ONE OF GOD'S CHILDREN WITHOUT DIRECT PERMISSION FROM GOD

This teaching is a conclusion drawn from limited information but not without Scriptural support. In other words, the Bible is not totally silent in this teaching. Therefore, I am not establishing a doctrine from silence or personal opinion. While every believer can potentially be subjected to demonic temptation and harassment, the major offensives coming from Satan or his demonic host can seemingly only be launched with permission from God.

We know from the Word of God that Satan and his cohorts prowl around looking for candidates to "devour."

> *1 Peter 5:8 (ESV) Be sober-minded; be watchful. Your adversary the devil prowls around like a roaring lion, seeking someone to devour.*

> *Job 1:7 (ESV) The LORD said to Satan, "From where have you come?" Satan answered the LORD and said, "From going to and fro on the earth, and from walking up and down on it."*

> *Job 2:2 (ESV) And the LORD said to Satan, "From where have you come?" Satan answered the LORD and said, "From going to and fro on the earth, and from walking up and down on it."*

It would seem that when believers are involved, the enemy needs to go before God to gain His permission before they can carry out their plans. This idea is precisely the picture given in the book of Job, which I believe is meant to provide a glimpse into the interactions between God and Satan that can potentially affect our lives. We will do an injustice to Biblical instruction if we limit the 42 chapters of Job as our example of having patience in trials. The Book of Job is filled with doctrinal teaching on a vast number of topics.

In his "roaming about on the earth," Satan had selected Job as a desired target. It was God who asked Satan if he had noticed his servant Job.

> **Job 1:8 (ESV) And the LORD said to Satan, "Have you considered my servant Job, that there is none like him on the earth, a blameless and upright man, who fears God and turns away from evil?"**

> **Job 2:3 (ESV) And the LORD said to Satan, "Have you considered my servant Job, that there is none like him on the earth, a blameless and upright man, who fears God and turns away from evil? He still holds fast his integrity, although you incited me against him to destroy him without reason."**

Satan revealed that he had noticed Job and then started his accusations against Job and God.

> **Job 1:9-10 (ESV) Then Satan answered the LORD and said, "Does Job fear God for no reason? 10 Have you not put a hedge around him and his house and all that he has, on every side? You have blessed the work of his hands, and his possessions have increased in the land.**

Satan wanted to destroy Job and have the servant of God curse his creator. However, he had to seek permission from God before he could execute his plan, which was to afflict Job with severe hardships to see how strong his faith in God really was. God granted that permission but set distinct bounds beyond which Satan could not go. The enemy had to operate under the sovereignty of God and abide by these restrictions.

> *Job 1:12 (ESV) And the LORD said to Satan, "Behold, all that he has is in your hand. Only against him do not stretch out your hand." So Satan went out from the presence of the LORD.*

> *Job 2:4-7 (ESV) Then Satan answered the LORD and said, "Skin for skin! All that a man has he will give for his life. 5 But stretch out your hand and touch his bone and his flesh, and he will curse you to your face." 6 And the LORD said to Satan, "Behold, he is in your hand; only spare his life." 7 So Satan went out from the presence of the LORD and struck Job with loathsome sores from the sole of his foot to the crown of his head.*

Satan was given permission to have Job's oxen and donkeys stolen. The Sabeans killed Job's servants, who kept the oxen and donkeys. Then fire fell from heaven and burned Job's sheep and the servants keeping them. Then the Chaldeans stole Job's camels and killed the servants keeping them. Then a wind blew down the house that all of Job's sons and daughters were in and destroyed them all. Despite all these tragic events caused by Satan, Job's response of praising God should be an example to us all.

Job 1:21 (ESV) And he said, "Naked I came from my mother's womb, and naked shall I return. The LORD gave, and the LORD has taken away; blessed be the name of the LORD."

What a testimony of faith from the righteous man.

Job 1:22 (ESV) In all this Job did not sin or charge God with wrong.

Another example in Scripture is Satan's request to God that he be allowed to "sift" Peter like wheat. Again, permission was granted to the enemy. However, Jesus stepped in with His prayers so that Satan's assault would not result in Peter's faith being lost.

Luke 22:31-32 (ESV) "Simon, Simon, behold, Satan demanded to have you, that he might sift you like wheat, 32 but I have prayed for you that your faith may not fail. And when you have turned again, strengthen your brothers."

We don't know God's criteria to determine whether He will grant Satan's requests to sift us somehow. It may have to do with the potential good God sees He can bring through the affliction or trial that Satan proposes. The Father knows if we will give Him glory, and His testimony will go forth through our lives. Paul testified that he wanted to glorify the Father in life or death. Paul struggled to stay on earth and preach the good news or leave his fleshly body through death to be with the Lord.

Philippians 1:21-23 (ESV) For to me to live is Christ, and to die is gain. 22 If I am to live in the flesh, that means fruitful labor for me. Yet which I shall choose I cannot tell. 23 I am hard pressed between the two. My desire is to depart and be with Christ, for that is far better.

When proactive and embracing suffering through rejoicing and praise, we grow in endurance, character, hope, and love. Paul and Silas learned this and were able to praise even while imprisoned.

Romans 5:3-5 (ESV) Not only that, but we rejoice in our sufferings, knowing that suffering produces endurance, 4 and endurance produces character, and character produces hope, 5 and hope does not put us to shame, because God's love has been poured into our hearts through the Holy Spirit who has been given to us.

Hebrews 12:10-11 (ESV) For they disciplined us for a short time as it seemed best to them, but he disciplines us for our good, that we may share his holiness. 11 For the moment all discipline seems painful rather than pleasant, but later it yields the peaceful fruit of righteousness to those who have been trained by it.

One of the keywords in James 1:2-4 is "when." The Scripture does not say "if" but "when" we meet trials of various kinds. We all will be tempted and tested by the enemy. We all will be persecuted for righteousness's sake if we walk with the Lord. Those who love God will be persecuted. We must count it all joy in temptations, trials, afflictions, and persecutions. The testing of our faith produces steadfastness, which leads to Christian maturity.

> ***James 1:2-4 (ESV) Count it all joy, my brothers, when you meet trials of various kinds, 3 for you know that the testing of your faith produces steadfastness. 4 And let steadfastness have its full effect, that you may be perfect and complete, lacking in nothing.***

Job and Peter reaped significant spiritual benefits from the trials of their faith that came from Satan's hand. God also allowed Satan to afflict Paul through his "thorn in the flesh" because it served God's purpose of keeping Paul from exalting himself after having the extraordinary privilege of visiting the third heaven.

> ***2 Corinthians 12:7-10 (ESV) So to keep me from becoming conceited because of the surpassing greatness of the revelations, a thorn was given me in the flesh, a messenger of Satan to harass me, to keep me from becoming conceited. 8 Three times I pleaded with the Lord about this, that it should leave me. 9 But he said to me, "My grace is sufficient for you, for my power is made perfect in weakness." Therefore I will boast all the more gladly of my weaknesses, so that the power of Christ may rest upon me. 10 For the sake of Christ, then, I am content with weaknesses, insults, hardships, persecutions, and calamities. For when I am weak, then I am strong.***

Questions For Chapter 23

1. Can Satan launch significant offensives against believers without permission from God?

2. What happened when Satan sought permission to target Job?

3. How did Job respond to the tragic events caused by Satan?

4. Was permission granted to Satan to sift Peter like wheat?

5. What benefits can come from trials and suffering?

Chapter 24
THE ENEMY CAN NOT CREATE ANYTHING

God is the author and creator of all things. The demonic are created beings and do not possess the power or authority to create or speak anything into existence. The Bible leaves no room for any source of creation other than the Godhead, strongly specifying that nothing else has ever come into being apart from Him. For your edification, I will post a few verses showing that God the Father, Son, and Holy Spirit created everything.

> *Genesis 1:1 (ESV) In the beginning, God created the heavens and the earth.*

> *Psalms 33:6 (ESV) By the word of the LORD the heavens were made, and by the breath of his mouth all their host.*

> *Psalms 102:25 (ESV) Of old you laid the foundation of the earth, and the heavens are the work of your hands.*

> *Isaiah 45:12 (ESV) I made the earth and created man on it; it was my hands that stretched out the heavens, and I commanded all their host.*

> *Isaiah 45:18 (ESV) For thus says the LORD, who created the heavens (he is God!), who formed the*

earth and made it (he established it; he did not create it empty, he formed it to be inhabited!): "I am the LORD, and there is no other.

John 1:3 (ESV) All things were made through him, and without him was not any thing made that was made.

Romans 11:36 (ESV) For from him and through him and to him are all things. To him be glory forever. Amen.

1 Corinthians 8:6 (ESV) yet for us there is one God, the Father, from whom are all things and for whom we exist, and one Lord, Jesus Christ, through whom are all things and through whom we exist.

Colossians 1:16-17 (ESV) For by him all things were created, in heaven and on earth, visible and invisible, whether thrones or dominions or rulers or authorities—all things were created through him and for him. 17 And he is before all things, and in him all things hold together.

Hebrews 1:2 (ESV) but in these last days he has spoken to us by his Son, whom he appointed the heir of all things, through whom also he created the world.

Revelation 4:11 (ESV) "Worthy are you, our Lord and God, to receive glory and honor and power, for you created all things, and by your will they existed and were created."

God's creative work includes time, space, matter, the visible and the invisible, and absolutely everything that exists in earthly and spiritual realms. In contrast, all that Satan can create are illusions and chaos.

Questions For Chapter 24

1. Who is the creator of all things, according to the Bible?

2. What does Genesis 1:1 state about the creation of the heavens and the earth?

3. What role did Jesus play in the creation of all things, according to Colossians 1:16-17?

4. How does God's creative work differ from what Satan can create?

5. According to Revelation 4:11, why is God worthy of glory, honor, and power?

Chapter 25
THE ENEMY CAN NOT OFFER REWARDS TO HIS FOLLOWERS

The enemy cannot offer peace or any hope of a joyful eternity. Only in the Godhead can we find the fruit of the Spirit, which is the character of who God is. God is love, joy, and peace. The enemy only knows how to lie, accuse, steal, and destroy the things God created. Galatians 5:19-21 gives us an example of the works of the enemy in and through people.

Galatians 5:19-21 (ESV) Now the works of the flesh are evident: sexual immorality, impurity, sensuality, 20 idolatry, sorcery, enmity, strife, jealousy, fits of anger, rivalries, dissensions, divisions, 21 envy, drunkenness, orgies, and things like these. I warn you, as I warned you before, that those who do such things will not inherit the kingdom of God.

In contrast to the works of the enemy in the lost person, Galatians 5:22-23 gives us the work of the Holy Spirit in the life of someone spiritually born again.

Galatians 5:22-23 (ESV) But the fruit of the Spirit is love, joy, peace, patience, kindness, goodness, faithfulness, 23 gentleness, self-control; against such things there is no law.

The work of our Lord was to destroy the works of the enemy so that we could walk in the peace and joy of the Father.

> **John 16:33 (ESV) I have said these things to you, that in me you may have peace. In the world you will have tribulation. But take heart; I have overcome the world."**

> **1 John 3:8 (ESV) Whoever makes a practice of sinning is of the devil, for the devil has been sinning from the beginning. The reason the Son of God appeared was to destroy the works of the devil.**

> **Romans 16:20 (ESV) The God of peace will soon crush Satan under your feet. The grace of our Lord Jesus Christ be with you.**

Nothing that Satan has to offer a man is genuinely satisfying. The enemy describes the pleasures he offers as he lures mankind to their beauty and great quality.

> **Genesis 3:1-6 (ESV) Now the serpent was more crafty than any other beast of the field that the LORD God had made. He said to the woman, "Did God actually say, 'You shall not eat of any tree in the garden'?" 2 And the woman said to the serpent, "We may eat of the fruit of the trees in the garden, 3 but God said, 'You shall not eat of the fruit of the tree that is in the midst of the garden, neither shall you touch it, lest you die.'" 4 But the serpent said to the woman, "You will not surely die. 5 For God knows that when you eat of it your eyes will be opened, and you will be like**

God, knowing good and evil." 6 So when the woman saw that the tree was good for food, and that it was a delight to the eyes, and that the tree was to be desired to make one wise, she took of its fruit and ate, and she also gave some to her husband who was with her, and he ate.

Matthew 4:8-9 (ESV) Again, the devil took him to a very high mountain and showed him all the kingdoms of the world and their glory. 9 And he said to him, "All these I will give you, if you will fall down and worship me."

However, those who follow after the demonic will ultimately discover the false nature of their promises. Those who follow the temptation will find themselves quickly sliding down a road that leads to despair and death rather than the glorious life they were promised.

Proverbs 14:12 (ESV) There is a way that seems right to a man, but its end is the way to death.

Matthew 7:13-14 (ESV) "Enter by the narrow gate. For the gate is wide and the way is easy that leads to destruction, and those who enter by it are many. 14 For the gate is narrow and the way is hard that leads to life, and those who find it are few.

Romans 6:23 (ESV) For the wages of sin is death, but the free gift of God is eternal life in Christ Jesus our Lord.

2 Corinthians 11:14-15 (ESV) And no wonder, for even Satan disguises himself as an angel of light.

15 So it is no surprise if his servants, also, disguise themselves as servants of righteousness. Their end will correspond to their deeds.

Questions For Chapter 25

1. What are the works of the enemy mentioned in Galatians 5:19-21?

2. What is the contrast between the works of the enemy and the work of the Holy Spirit?

3. What was the purpose of the Son of God appearing, according to 1 John 3:8?

4. What did Satan offer to Jesus in Matthew 4:8-9?

5. What is the ultimate consequence of following after the demonic, according to Romans 6:23?

Chapter 26
THE ENEMY CANNOT SNATCH THE REDEEMED AWAY FROM GOD

We are saved by faith and kept by faith. Nothing outside of having a faithless heart can cause a Christian to leave the place of salvation. When a person puts his faith in Jesus Christ's death on the cross for the forgiveness of his sins, he enters into a covenant relationship with God that is anchored in the shed blood of Jesus and sealed with God's oath. No other being outside of the individual has the spiritual authority to supersede this divine act of covenant and cancel this covenant between God and man. No matter how great Satan and his demons may affect a believer or how far he may lead a believer astray, the enemy cannot nullify a believer's salvation. In this study, we discussed in detail what the enemy can and cannot do. We gave warnings to believers from the Scriptures. The enemy is on the prowl, seeking whom he may devour. We must walk in the Spirit and be a people of faith in God and His Word. Let's close this teaching with some great truths concerning the anchor of our hope.

> *John 10:27-29 (ESV) My sheep hear my voice, and I know them, and they follow me. 28 I give them eternal life, and they will never perish, and no one will snatch them out of my hand. 29 My Father, who has given them to me, is greater than all, and no one is able to snatch them out of the Father's hand.*

Questions For Chapter 26

1. What is the basis for a Christian's salvation and the assurance of being kept in the place of salvation?

2. How is the covenant relationship between a believer and God established and secured?

3. Can any external force or spiritual being nullify or cancel the covenant between God and a believer?

4. Can the enemy (Satan) nullify a believer's salvation or cause them to lose it?

5. What assurance does Jesus give to His followers regarding their eternal security?

Chapter 27
JESUS: THE ANCHOR OF OUR SOUL

We know from Hebrews 6:17-20 the doctrine of the immutability of God. This word immutability means that our Father is unchanging. His character is unchangeable, and in that, God cannot lie. The fact that God is not a man that He should lie is a sure and steadfast anchor for our souls.

Hebrews 6:17-20 ESV So when God desired to show more convincingly to the heirs of the promise the unchangeable character of his purpose, he guaranteed it with an oath, (18) so that by two unchangeable things, in which it is impossible for God to lie, we who have fled for refuge might have strong encouragement to hold fast to the hope set before us. (19) We have this as a sure and steadfast anchor of the soul, a hope that enters into the inner place behind the curtain, (20) where Jesus has gone as a forerunner on our behalf, having become a high priest forever after the order of Melchizedek.

We know from Hebrews 8:6-7 that if the Old Covenant were good for the salvation of mankind, there would have been no need for the New Covenant. In the New Covenant, we have a relationship and fellowship with the Father built on a foundation with better promises. Therefore, we have the choice of who sits at our table. Because of our sonship through the New Covenant, we have been authority over the enemy, and the Father has given us the keys to the Kingdom and victory.

> ***Hebrews 8:6-7 ESV   But as it is, Christ has obtained a ministry that is as much more excellent than the old as the covenant he mediates is better, since it is enacted on better promises. (7) For if that first covenant had been faultless, there would have been no occasion to look for a second.***

We know from Hebrews 9:15-17 that a will has been written out, leaving us a beneficiary of the promises. First, the one who owned everything (our Lord Jesus Christ) had to die before the will could be enacted, which He did. Then we needed a lawyer or mediator to stand on our behalf to ensure we received the promises written out in the will. The enemy seeks to keep us from the promises of the will and rob us of our inheritance. Our Lord Jesus rose from the dead, ascended back into heaven, and sat down at the Father's right hand to mediate as our lawyer to ensure we received the promises.

> ***Hebrews 9:15-17 ESV   Therefore he is the mediator of a new covenant, so that those who are called may receive the promised eternal inheritance, since a death has occurred that redeems them from the transgressions committed under the first covenant. (16) For where a will is involved, the death of the one who made it must be established. (17) For a will takes effect only at death, since it is not in force as long as the one who made it is alive.***

We have a greater Covenant with better promises, and our Lord has empowered us with His Holy Spirit, which lives within us. Greater is He (the Holy Spirit) than he (Satan and the demonic) who is in the world. We must approach the ministry and mandate of spiritual warfare with the knowledge and attitude that we are more than conquerors in Christ Jesus our Lord. We can walk in total deliverance from any form of demonization or strongholds. We stand without excuse because God has given us victory.

> **1 John 4:4 ESV Little children, you are from God and have overcome them, for he who is in you is greater than he who is in the world.**

Because of a heart of faith in God and His Word, through the shed blood of our Lord Jesus Christ, we know with complete assurance we have eternal life.

> **1 John 5:13 ESV I write these things to you who believe in the name of the Son of God that you may know that you have eternal life.**

In the New Covenant, we have the Biblical assurance that we can hear the Shepherd's voice, and we will follow Him. We are saved by faith and kept by faith. No one put us in the hands of the Father, and no one outside of ourselves can remove us from the hands of our Father.

> **John 10:27-29 ESV My sheep hear my voice, and I know them, and they follow me. (28) I give them eternal life, and they will never perish, and no one will snatch them out of my hand. (29) My Father, who has given them to me, is greater than all, and**

no one is able to snatch them out of the Father's hand.

What have we read in this study? Yes, we are called into a life of spiritual warfare. Yes, we can be heavily influenced by the forces of the demonic. But we can walk in the victory of our enemies. We are commanded to know the schemes of the enemy. Ignoring the demonic and their activity around us will not cause them to act harmlessly or flee from us. Satan and his demonic host are fallen angels who hate God and His children. They are enemies of God and the Kingdom of Heaven. Therefore, they are our enemies. The forces of darkness seek out God's children to tempt them to curse and deny God.

The demonic forces are limited by the will of God in that they cannot do what He does not allow. They are also limited by time and space. We might not understand the dynamics of created spirit beings, and maybe we can't wrap our minds around what form they might manifest themselves. However, we know they can only be in one place at a time. We know there are no more demons today than when God created the heavens and earth. They cannot procreate, nor can they die. The number has remained the same, and their power has remained the same.

However, we serve the Lord God of Abraham, Isaac, and Jacob, who is omnipresent, omniscient, and omnipotent. It is hope to the soul knowing that our God is all-present, all-knowing, and all-powerful. No temptation the enemy can throw at me that is not common to mankind because there is nothing new under the sun. There is no temptation so great that God has not given me a way to escape it if I want to walk as an overcomer instead of a victim.

1 Corinthians 10:13 (ESV) No temptation has overtaken you that is not common to man. God is faithful, and he will not let you be tempted beyond your ability, but with the temptation he will also provide the way of escape, that you may be able to endure it.

Take a glance at the demonic and know they are there planning and scheming against you and your family but set your face towards the King of Glory. Know that greater is He that is in you than he that is in the world. Walk by faith, speak by faith, draw near to God, and resist the devil, and he must flee from you. Know this. There will be times of darkness that seem like we are walking to our death. However, it is only a shadow, and we have no reason to fear because the Shepherd is with us, and His rod and staff comfort us.

Psalms 23:4 (ESV) Even though I walk through the valley of the shadow of death, I will fear no evil, for you are with me; your rod and your staff, they comfort me.

Our God has prepared a table for us in the presence of our enemies. He did not say they would sit at the table with us but was forced to watch us. So don't invite the enemy to sit at your table by your words and deeds. Allow the Father to anoint your head until your cup overflows in His presence.

Psalms 23:5 (ESV) You prepare a table before me in the presence of my enemies; you anoint my head with oil; my cup overflows.

We have a promise when we walk in the New Covenant relationship with the Father. His goodness and mercy will follow us all the days of our life, and we will build a habitation for His presence.

Psalms 23:6 (ESV) Surely goodness and mercy shall follow me all the days of my life, and I shall dwell in the house of the LORD forever.

I pray for you as you have been through this teaching that you will walk in the mental, emotional, physical, relational, and spiritual freedom the Father has promised you in His Son through the indwelling Holy Spirit. Be free and choose this day who will sit at your table.

Questions For Chapter 27

1. What is the significance of the immutability of God mentioned in Hebrews 6:17-20?

2. Why was there a need for the New Covenant according to Hebrews 8:6-7?

3. How does Hebrews 9:15-17 explain the process of receiving the promises of the will?

4. What assurance do believers have regarding their victory over the enemy?

5. What does 1 Corinthians 10:13 teach us about facing temptations?

WORKBOOK QUESTIONS AND ANSWERS

ANSWERS FOR CHAPTER 1

1. How should we establish true doctrine when it comes to spiritual warfare?
   Answer: All experiences must be found in the Old Testament's shadow and the New Testament's substance.

2. Was casting out demons limited to first-century Christians?
   Answer: No, all believers are called to cast out demons.

3. Is spiritual warfare limited to a unique gifting or calling among believers?
   Answer: No, all believers are called to engage in spiritual warfare.

4. What examples from the Bible can we draw upon to understand the teaching of demonic activity?
   Answer: The Bible provides examples of Jesus and His disciples casting out demons.

5. What authority do believers have in helping others with spiritual demonic strongholds?
   Answer: Believers have the authority to help others through prayer, deliverance, and the power of the Holy Spirit.

ANSWERS FOR CHAPTER 2

7. What is the author's perspective on people who deny the existence or activity of demons?

Answer: The author believes that those who deny the existence or activity of demons are deceived by a demonic spirit and blinded to the truth.

8. Why does the author consider the attitude of "out of sight, out of mind" towards demons dangerous?
Answer: The author views the "out of sight, out of mind" attitude as dangerous because demons' activity is not influenced by our belief in them or our attempts to ignore them. The demons can still bother and influence individuals regardless of their awareness or acknowledgment.

9. How does the author describe the impact of deception?
Answer: The author states that the most significant problem with deception is that people often don't realize they are deceived. Deception is described as deceivingly deceptive, which can lead individuals to believe they are not being deceived while the enemy continues to deceive them.

10. According to 2 Timothy 3:1-7, what will people's behavior be in the last days?
Answer: According to the Apostle Paul's words in 2 Timothy 3:1-7, people in the last days will exhibit various negative traits such as being lovers of self, lovers of money, proud, arrogant, abusive, disobedient, ungrateful, heartless, slanderous, without self-control, brutal, treacherous, reckless, and lovers of pleasure rather than lovers of God. They may also have the appearance of godliness but deny its power.

11. How does the author reassure the readers regarding the enemy's schemes?
Answer: The author assures the readers that the cross and the blood of the Lamb shed for them is enough to defeat the enemy's schemes. Despite the enemy's plans to do evil, God has a plan to bless individuals and turn evil into good.

ANSWERS FOR CHAPTER 3

1. What does it mean to put on the whole armor of God?
    Answer: It refers to being prepared and equipped for spiritual warfare.

2. According to the text, what is one of the characteristics of the enemy described as a roaring lion?
    Answer: One characteristic of the enemy, described as a roaring lion, is his intention to seek someone to devour.

3. Why does the author emphasize the importance of putting on the whole armor of God?
    Answer: The author emphasizes the importance of putting on the whole armor of God to be prepared and equipped for spiritual warfare against the enemy's schemes.

4. How does the author refute the notion that the enemy is toothless and harmless?
    Answer: The author refutes the notion by highlighting the warnings in Scripture, such as 1 Peter 5:8-9, that describe the enemy as a roaring lion seeking to devour and cause suffering. The author suggests that the enemy's activity does not align with being harmless.

5. What does the author propose as a crucial element in defeating the schemes of Satan, according to 2 Corinthians 2:10-11?
    Answer: The author proposes forgiveness as a vital element in defeating the schemes of Satan, as stated by the Apostle Paul. Forgiveness prevents believers from being outwitted by Satan and his designs.

6. How does Satan deceive people, as mentioned in 2 Corinthians 11:13-14?
   Answer: Satan deceives people by disguising himself as an angel of light. This disguising allows him to deceive individuals by calling good evil and evil good, leading them astray from the truth.

ANSWERS FOR CHAPTER 4

1. How can the demonic affect a person's walk with the Lord?
   Answer: The demonic can influence and tempt believers to sin.

2. What authority do believers have when it comes to dealing with demons?
   Answer: Believers have authority in the name of Jesus to cast out demons.

3. Is spiritual warfare a spiritual gift or a mandate for all believers?
   Answer: It is a mandate for all believers to engage in spiritual warfare and cast out demons

4. According to Mark 16, what is the sign/signs that follow a true believer in Christ?
   a) Speaking in new tongues
   b) Performing miracles
   c) Casting out demons
   d) All of the above
   Answer: d) All of the above

5. How did our Lord Jesus Christ cast out demons, according to Matthew 8:16?
   a) By screaming at them
   b) By using physical force

c) By speaking a simple word with authority

d) By praying for hours

Answer: c) By speaking a simple word with authority

ANSWERS FOR CHAPTER 5

1. According to Hebrews 2:14, what did Jesus accomplish through His death?

    Answer: Through His death, Jesus destroyed the one who has the power of death, which is the devil.

2. What does Matthew 16:19 suggest about the authority given to believers?

    Answer: Matthew 16:19 states that believers are given the keys of the kingdom of heaven, with the power to bind and loose things on earth and have corresponding effects in heaven.

3. In Revelation 1:17-18, what does Jesus declare about Himself?

    Answer: Jesus declares that He is the first and the last, the living one who died and is alive forevermore, and that He holds the keys of Death and Hades.

4. What assurance is given in 2 Thessalonians 3:3 regarding believers' protection?

    Answer: 2 Thessalonians 3:3 assures believers that the Lord is faithful and will establish and guard them against the evil one.

ANSWERS FOR CHAPTER 6

6. Does the Bible explicitly state whether a Christian can have a demon?

Answer: No, the Bible does not explicitly state whether a Christian can have a demon.

7. What does the term "offended" mean in Matthew 11:6?
Answer: In this context, "offended" means being tripped up or stumbling over something.

8. Why is it important to distinguish between the innermost man (spirit) and the inner man (soul)?
Answer: It is essential because while the Holy Spirit dwells in the innermost man (spirit), the inner man (soul) battles daily with sin.

9. Should theological teachings be based solely on personal experiences?
Answer: No, theological teachings should be based on the Word of God rather than personal experiences.

10. How does the lack of explicit biblical texts for certain doctrines pose a danger?
Answer: The lack of explicit biblical texts for certain doctrines can lead to interpreting isolated texts based on personal experiences or passing on doctrinal beliefs without a solid biblical foundation.

ANSWERS FOR CHAPTER 7

6. Were believers in the Old Testament saved by the law or by faith?
Answer: Believers in the Old Testament were saved by faith, not by the law.

7. Where did the souls and spirits of Old Testament believers go when they died?

Answer: The souls and spirits of Old Testament believers went to Abraham's bosom, waiting for the promise of our Lord Jesus Christ.

8. What does Romans 4:1-6 teach us about righteousness and faith?
    Answer: Romans 4:1-6 teaches us that righteousness is counted to those who believe in God by faith, not by works.

9. What was the purpose of the Old Testament sacrificial system?
    Answer: The purpose of the Old Testament sacrificial system was to point to the future shedding of blood by the Son of God for the sinful human race.

10. How did Abraham demonstrate his faith according to Romans 4:9-22?
    Answer: Abraham demonstrated his faith by believing in God's promises, even when circumstances seemed impossible, and his faith was counted to him as righteousness.

ANSWERS FOR CHAPTER 8

6. What was the primary message preached by Jesus during the first three years of His ministry?
    Answer: The primary message preached by Jesus during the first three years of His ministry was the gospel of the kingdom of heaven, which focused on the rule and reign of God in the hearts and lives of believers.

7. When did Jesus begin to preach about His death, burial, and resurrection?

Answer: Jesus began to preach about His death, burial, and resurrection around His third year of ministry.

8. How did Peter initially react to Jesus' message about His death?
Answer: Peter took Jesus aside and rebuked Him, saying that such a thing should never happen to Him.

9. What did Jesus say in response to Peter's statement?
Answer: Jesus turned to Peter and said, "Get behind me, Satan! You are a hindrance to me. For you are not setting your mind on the things of God, but on the things of man."

10. When did the disciples come to believe in the resurrection of Jesus?
Answer: The disciples came to believe in the resurrection of Jesus after His post-resurrection appearances. Initially, when Jesus died, they thought all hope was lost and did not understand or believe in His resurrection.

ANSWERS FOR CHAPTER 9

6. What did the thief on the cross say to Jesus?
Answer: The thief said, "Jesus, remember me when you come into your kingdom."

7. How did Jesus respond to the thief on the cross?
Answer: Jesus responded, "Truly, I say to you, today you will be with me in Paradise."

8. What was the physical condition of Jesus while the thief was placing his trust in Him?

Answer: Jesus was beaten, bloody, and gasping for every breath, with blood pouring from His head, back, face, and hands.

9. How did the thief's salvation resemble the salvation of Old Testament saints?
Answer: Like the Old Testament saints, the thief believed in God and had righteousness imputed upon him.

10. What is Paradise referred to as in the context of the waiting place for believers who died before the cross?
Answer: Paradise is called Abraham's bosom, where all who had believed and died from Adam to the moment of the cross awaited their final destination.

ANSWERS FOR CHAPTER 10

6. What did Jesus command the disciples when He appeared to them after His resurrection?
Answer: Jesus commanded the disciples, "Receive you the Holy Spirit."

7. Were the disciples already believers before they received the Holy Spirit?
Answer: Yes, the disciples were already believers and had put their trust and faith in Jesus Christ.

8. What did Jesus mean when He said the Holy Spirit would be "in" the disciples?
Answer: Jesus meant that the Holy Spirit would come and dwell within the disciples, becoming an indwelling presence.

9. How did the disciples' experience of receiving the Holy Spirit fulfill a command from Jesus in John chapter 7?
Answer: In John chapter 7, Jesus spoke about the Spirit, whom those who believed in Him would receive. The disciples received the Holy Spirit, fulfilling this command.

10. In John 16:7, why did Jesus tell the disciples that it was to their advantage for Him to go away?
Answer: Jesus explained that the Helper (the Holy Spirit) would not come to them if He did not go away. His departure was necessary for the Holy Spirit to be sent to them.

ANSWERS FOR CHAPTER 11

6. What command from Luke 24:49 did Jesus give the disciples before the outpouring of the Holy Spirit?
Answer: Jesus commanded the disciples to go into the upper room in Jerusalem and wait until they were endued with power.

7. Who is responsible for baptizing believers with the Holy Spirit?
Answer: It is the job of our Lord Jesus Christ to baptize believers with the Holy Spirit.

8. What was the significance of the event in Acts chapter 2 for the believers?
Answer: In Acts chapter 2, the believers experienced the outpouring of the Holy Spirit, fulfilling the prophetic word of John the Baptist, and received the power of the Holy Spirit.

9. How did the disciples' experience in Acts chapter 2 differ from their state before that event?
    Answer: Before Acts chapter 2, the disciples were already believers with the Holy Spirit dwelling within them, but in Acts chapter 2, they received a special empowerment and filling of the Holy Spirit.

10. When did the indwelling of the Holy Spirit begin for believers, according to the Bible?
    Answer: The indwelling of the Holy Spirit for believers began after Jesus' resurrection, specifically in John 20:22, when Jesus breathed on the disciples and said, "Receive the Holy Spirit."

ANSWERS FOR CHAPTER 12

6. Who vowed to give her son to the Lord to serve Him all his life?
    Answer: Hannah, the wife of Elkanah.

7. Who anointed Saul as the King of Israel?
    Answer: Samuel the Prophet.

8. Why did Samuel rebuke Saul?
    Answer: Saul offered unlawful sacrifices, disobeying the command of the Lord.

9. Why did God reject Saul as king?
    Answer: Saul rejected the word of the Lord and did what was evil in His sight.

10. What happened to Saul after the Spirit of the Lord departed from him?
    Answer: He was tormented by a harmful spirit sent by the Lord.

ANSWERS FOR CHAPTER 13

6. According to Matthew 10:1-4, what authority did Jesus give his twelve disciples?
Answer: Jesus gave his twelve disciples authority over unclean spirits, to cast them out, and to heal every disease and affliction.

7. In Matthew 4:10, who did Jesus address as "Satan"?
Answer: Jesus addressed Satan when He said, "Be gone, Satan!" It was in response to Satan's temptation during Jesus' time in the wilderness.

8. Who was the "daughter of Abraham" mentioned in Luke 13:11-17, and what did Jesus do for her?
Answer: The "daughter of Abraham" was a woman who had a disabling spirit for eighteen years. Jesus healed her by casting out the demon, and she was immediately made straight.

9. In Acts 5:1-6, why did Peter rebuke Ananias, and what was the consequence of his actions?
Answer: Peter rebuked Ananias for lying to the Holy Spirit by keeping back a portion of the proceeds from selling his property. As a result, Ananias fell down and breathed his last.

10. According to 1 Corinthians 5:1-5, what action did Paul instruct the Corinth church to take regarding a man guilty of sexual immorality?
Answer: Paul instructed the Corinth church to put the man guilty of sexual immorality out of the church and deliver him to Satan for the destruction of the flesh,

hoping that his spirit would be saved in the day of the Lord.

ANSWERS FOR CHAPTER 14

6. Is the ministry of "casting out demons" limited to a select group of spiritual warriors chosen by God?
   Answer: No, all believers are called to participate in the deliverance ministry.

7. Do some people overlook or ignore the concept of "spiritual warfare"?
   Answer: Yes, some individuals may disregard or disregard anything related to spiritual warfare.

8. Is the term "deliverance ministry" often associated with horror movies?
   Answer: It may be, but in reality, it refers to the practice of freeing individuals from demonic oppression.

9. Is "deliverance ministry" exclusively performed by charismatic Christians?
   Answer: No, deliverance ministry is not limited to any specific Christian denomination or group.

10. According to Jesus' teachings, is casting out demons an act of faith?
    Answer: Yes, Jesus taught that casting out demons requires faith and that nothing is impossible for those who have faith, even as small as a mustard seed.

ANSWERS FOR CHAPTER 15

6. Can the enemy operate outside the bounds of God's sovereignty? Why? Explain.
Answer: No, the enemy, Satan, cannot operate outside the bounds of God's sovereignty. He always reports to the One who created him.

7. Does God possess unlimited knowledge, presence, and power?
Answer: Yes, God has no limitation in knowledge, presence, or power. He is omnipresent, omniscient, and omnipotent.

8. What is the status of the fallen angels who followed the devil?
Answer: The fallen angels who followed the devil still maintain the status of being created spirits. They are limited in time, space, matter, authority, and power.

9. Is Satan all-knowing and all-powerful like God?
Answer: No, Satan is not all-knowing or all-powerful. He and the demons cannot be in more than one place at a time, contrary to what some may think.

10. How can a believer open the door to the influence of demons?
Answer: A believer can open the door to the demonic through sins of commission (doing known sins) or sins of omission (neglecting to do what is good or neglecting daily biblical disciplines).

ANSWERS FOR CHAPTER 16

6. Does Satan still have access to come before God and accuse mankind?

Answer: Yes, according to Job 1:6, Satan still has access to come before God and accuse mankind.

7. What did God point out to Satan about Job in Job 1:8?
Answer: God praised Job's faith and devotion, pointing out that there was none like him on earth, a blameless and upright man who feared God and turned away from evil.

8. What revelation did the enemy make about God's blessings upon Job in Job 1:10?
Answer: The enemy testified that God had put a hedge of protection around Job and his house, blessed the work of his hands, and increased his possessions in the land.

9. What authority did God give to the enemy in Job 1:12?
Answer: God allowed the enemy to have authority over all that Job possessed, but he was not allowed to stretch out his hand against Job himself.

10. Did God give the enemy complete, unwatched control over Job?
Answer: No, God limited what the enemy could do to Job by specifying that he could not stretch out his hand against Job himself.

ANSWERS FOR CHAPTER 17

6. Who was standing at the right hand of Joshua in Zechariah 3:1?
Answer: Satan

7. What does the phrase "the angel of the Lord" represent in the Old Testament?

Answer: The pre-incarnate Lord Jesus Christ

8. Why did Joshua remain silent while standing before the Lord in filthy garments?
Answer: It is unclear, but he may have felt awe and shame in the presence of God.

9. What did the Lord declare to Joshua in Zechariah 3:4?
Answer: The Lord said, "Behold, I have taken your iniquity away from you, and I will clothe you with pure vestments."

10. What condition was Joshua in before his transformation in Zechariah 3?
Answer: Joshua was clothed in filthy garments, representing sin and corruption.

ANSWERS FOR CHAPTER 18

6. Who was the spirit that came forward in 1 Kings 22:19-21, and what did he propose to do?
Answer: The spirit that came forward was an evil lying spirit. He proposed to entice Ahab to go up and fall at Ramoth-gilead.

7. In 1 Kings 22:22, what did the Lord ask the evil spirit, and how did the evil spirit respond?
Answer: The Lord asked the evil spirit, "By what means?" The evil spirit responded by saying that he would go out and be a lying spirit in the mouth of all Ahab's prophets, enticing him and ensuring his success.

8. In John 13:27-30, who entered Judas, and what did Jesus say to him?

Answer: Satan entered Judas, and Jesus said to him, "What you are going to do, do quickly."

9. What did God do in 1 Kings 22:23 regarding the lying spirit and the prophets?
    Answer: God put a lying spirit in the mouth of all Ahab's prophets, and the Lord declared disaster for Ahab.

10. According to 2 Thessalonians 2:9-12, why does God send a strong delusion, and who does it affect?
    Answer: God sends a strong delusion to those who refuse to love the truth and be saved. It affects those who did not believe the truth but took pleasure in unrighteousness.

ANSWERS FOR CHAPTER 19

1. What is the significance of studying the opponent's strengths and weaknesses in spiritual warfare?
    Answer: Studying the opponent's strengths and weaknesses in spiritual warfare is essential to effectively combat the enemy and avoid becoming unbalanced or devoting excessive time to the demonic forces. By understanding the strategies and tactics of Satan and his demons, individuals can be better equipped to counter their actions and remain balanced in their approach.

2. What is the role of Satan and his demonic forces in the lives of spiritually lost people?
    Answer: According to Ephesians 2:1-3, spiritually lost people naturally follow Satan and engage in his deeds. They are described as walking in the course of the world and being influenced by the prince of the power

of the air, who is the spirit at work in the Sons of Disobedience. Their lives are characterized by indulging in the passions of the flesh and carrying out the desires of the body and mind.

3. How does Satan blind the minds of unbelievers?
Answer: In 2 Corinthians 4:3-4, it is explained that the god of this world (referring to Satan) blinds the minds of unbelievers, preventing them from seeing the light of the gospel and the glory of Christ. We should know that Satan and his demonic host work to keep the truth of God's love and redemption veiled from those who are perishing. This deception hinders them from understanding and accepting the message of salvation.

4. Who are believers instructed to fight against in spiritual warfare?
Answer: According to Ephesians 6:12, believers are not called to fight against flesh and blood but against the rulers, authorities, and cosmic powers over this present darkness and the spiritual forces of evil in the heavenly places. Paul emphasizes that the battle is against demonic forces rather than human adversaries or fellow believers.

5. What is the purpose of putting on the whole armor of God in spiritual warfare?
Answer: Putting on the whole armor of God, as described in Ephesians 6:13-18, enables believers to withstand and stand firm in the face of evil and demonic forces. The armor includes the belt of truth, the breastplate of righteousness, shoes of readiness from the gospel of peace, the shield of faith, the helmet of salvation, and the sword of the Spirit (the Word of God). By equipping themselves with these spiritual

defenses, believers can effectively resist the devil's schemes and remain steadfast in their faith.

ANSWERS FOR CHAPTER 20

1. What does it mean to be born anew as children of a Holy God?
   Answer: Being born anew as children of a Holy God refers to the spiritual transformation that occurs when people accept Jesus Christ as their Savior and receive the imperishable seed of God's Word and the Holy Spirit within them.

2. How does the seed of Christ within us give rise to our new nature?
   Answer: The seed of Christ within us gives rise to our new nature by replicating the righteousness and holiness of our heavenly Father. As our old Adamic nature is crucified in Christ, our new nature is formed through the transformative power of God's living and abiding Word.

3. Which parts of a Christian can the demonic affect?
   Answer: The demonic can affect the soulish man of a Christian, which includes their thoughts (mind), emotions (feelings), and will (choices). Additionally, the demonic can also influence the physical body. These areas were subject to the enemy's dominion due to Adam and Eve's original sin.

4. What does it mean to walk in the Spirit, and why is it important?
   Answer: Walking in the Spirit refers to living a life guided by the Holy Spirit, where one sets their mind on the things of the Spirit and submits to God's law. It is

important because a life lived in the flesh, driven by worldly desires, is hostile to God and cannot please Him. Walking in the Spirit leads to life and peace.

5. How does teaching play a role in a believer's walk with the Lord?
   Answer: Teaching is crucial in a believer's walk with the Lord. Being taught the truth about Christ and His teachings is essential for spiritual growth and transformation. Pastors and teachers who dare to teach the truth are instrumental in guiding believers and helping them put off the old-man, be renewed in their minds, and put on the new-man created in the likeness of God.

ANSWERS FOR CHAPTER 21

1. Can the enemy make us engage in immoral acts?
   Answer: No, the enemy cannot make us engage in immoral acts. While the enemy can lead us to sinful waters and tempt us, we are ultimately responsible for our choices and actions.

2. What role does lust play in the process of temptation?
   Answer: Lust within our hearts is the starting point of every temptation. When we are lured and enticed by our own desires, temptation takes hold. It is important to recognize and address the desires of our hearts to prevent them from leading us into sin.

3. Does God tempt people with evil?
   Answer: No, God does not tempt people with evil. James 1:13 states that God cannot be tempted with evil, and He Himself tempts no one. Temptation originates

from our own desires and external influences but not from God.

4. How does God help us in the face of temptation?
    Answer: God is faithful and provides a way to escape every temptation. 1 Corinthians 10:13 assures us that no temptation is beyond our ability to resist, and with the temptation, God also provides a means for us to endure it.

5. What are the plans of the Father for our lives?
    Answer: According to Jeremiah 29:11, the plans of the Father for us are plans for welfare, not evil. He desires to give us a future and hope, indicating that His intentions are for our well-being and a blessed future.

ANSWERS FOR CHAPTER 22

1. Can evil demonic beings execute their will in a person's life without permission?
    Answer: No, evil demonic beings cannot execute their will in a person's life unless that person voluntarily relinquishes control to them. Unless a person has willfully chosen to enter a covenant relationship with such beings, they cannot automatically exert their influence.

2. How can demonic beings be connected to a person's life?
    Answer: Demonic beings can be connected to a person's life if that person has legal grounds or generational inheritances that allow for such connections. However, even with these connections, the demonic cannot act out in a person's life without

permission granted by the individual through acts of sin.

3. What is the purpose of Christian freedom according to Galatians 5:13?
    Answer: The purpose of Christian freedom, as stated in Galatians 5:13, is not to provide an opportunity for the flesh or worldly living. Instead, Christians are called to serve one another through love.

4. How should giving to the work of the ministry be approached?
    Answer: Giving to the work of the ministry should not be done out of compulsion or guilt but should result from the leadership of the Holy Spirit upon an individual's will. Philemon 1:14 emphasizes the importance of giving willingly and voluntarily.

5. How should believers walk in their freedom according to James 2:12?
    Answer: Believers should speak and act as those to be judged under the law of liberty, which is the freedom of God's grace. They should not revert to living under the yoke of the Law and sin, as warned by Paul in Galatians 5:1.

ANSWERS FOR CHAPTER 23

1. Can Satan launch major offensives against believers without permission from God?
    Answer: No, it would seem that when believers are involved, the enemy needs to seek permission from God before carrying out major offensives. The book of Job provides a glimpse into the interactions between

God and Satan, where Satan had to seek permission from God to afflict Job.

2. What happened when Satan sought permission to target Job?
    Answer: When Satan sought permission to target Job, God granted him limited permission but set distinct bounds beyond which Satan could not go. Satan was allowed to afflict Job with severe hardships to test his faith, but he had to operate under the sovereignty of God and abide by these restrictions.

3. How did Job respond to the tragic events caused by Satan?
    Answer: Despite all the tragic events caused by Satan, Job responded by praising God. He acknowledged that everything he had was given by the Lord and that the Lord had the authority to take it away. Job did not sin or charge God with wrongdoing.

4. Was permission granted to Satan to sift Peter like wheat?
    Answer: Yes, Satan demanded permission from God to sift Peter like wheat, and permission was granted. However, Jesus interceded through His prayers for Peter, ensuring that Peter's faith would not be lost.

5. What benefits can come from trials and suffering?
    Answer: Trials and suffering can produce endurance, character, hope, and love in the lives of believers. They can lead to Christian maturity and the development of steadfastness. Job and Peter experienced significant spiritual benefits from their trials, and even Paul saw the purpose of his "thorn in the flesh" as serving God's greater purpose.

ANSWERS FOR CHAPTER 24

1. Who is the creator of all things, according to the Bible?
   Answer: God, specifically the Godhead (Father, Son, and Holy Spirit), is the creator of all things.

2. What does Genesis 1:1 state about the creation of the heavens and the earth?
   Answer: Genesis 1:1 states that in the beginning, God created the heavens and the earth.

3. What role did Jesus play in the creation of all things, according to Colossians 1:16-17?
   Answer: Colossians 1:16-17 states that Jesus created all things, visible and invisible, in heaven and on earth. All things were created through Him and for Him.

4. How does God's creative work differ from what Satan can create?
   Answer: God's creative work encompasses everything in existence, including time, space, matter, and earthly and spiritual realms. On the other hand, Satan can only create illusions and chaos.

5. According to Revelation 4:11, why is God worthy of glory, honor, and power?
   Answer: Revelation 4:11 states that God is worthy of glory, honor, and power because He created all things, and they existed and were created by His will.

ANSWERS FOR CHAPTER 25

1. What are the works of the enemy mentioned in Galatians 5:19-21?

Answer: The works of the enemy mentioned in Galatians 5:19-21 include sexual immorality, impurity, sensuality, idolatry, sorcery, enmity, strife, jealousy, fits of anger, rivalries, dissensions, divisions, envy, drunkenness, orgies, and similar behaviors.

2. What is the contrast between the works of the enemy and the work of the Holy Spirit?
   Answer: The works of the enemy are characterized by sinful behaviors and destructive actions, while the work of the Holy Spirit produces the fruit of the Spirit, such as love, joy, peace, patience, kindness, goodness, faithfulness, gentleness, and self-control.

3. What was the purpose of the Son of God appearing, according to 1 John 3:8?
   Answer: The Son of God appeared to destroy the devil's works. His mission was to overcome and defeat the works of the enemy.

4. What did Satan offer to Jesus in Matthew 4:8-9?
   Answer: Satan offered to give Jesus all the kingdoms of the world and their glory if Jesus would worship him.

5. What is the ultimate consequence of following after the demonic, according to Romans 6:23?
   Answer: The wages of sin are death. Following the temptation and pursuing a path influenced by the enemy leads to despair and spiritual death.

ANSWERS FOR CHAPTER 26

1. What is the basis for a Christian's salvation and the assurance of being kept in the place of salvation?

Answer: The basis for a Christian's salvation and the assurance of being kept in the place of salvation is faith in Jesus Christ's death on the cross for the forgiveness of sins.

2. How is the covenant relationship between a believer and God established and secured?
    Answer: The covenant relationship between a believer and God is established and secured through faith in Jesus Christ's sacrificial death, which is anchored in His shed blood and sealed with God's oath.

3. Can any external force or being nullify or cancel the covenant between God and a believer?
    Answer: No, no other being outside of the individual has the spiritual authority to supersede or cancel the divine act of covenant between God and man. The covenant remains intact.

4. Can the enemy (Satan) nullify a believer's salvation or cause them to lose it?
    Answer: No, the enemy cannot nullify a believer's salvation or cause them to lose it. Once a person enters into a covenant relationship with God through faith, they are eternally secure, and no one can snatch them out of Jesus' or the Father's hand. They are put there by faith and kept there by faith.

5. What assurance does Jesus give to His followers regarding their eternal security?
    Answer: Jesus assures His followers that He gives them eternal life and they will never perish. No one will be able to snatch them out of His hand or the Father's hand. The Father, who is greater than all, safeguards their salvation.

ANSWERS FOR CHAPTER 27

1. What is the significance of the immutability of God
   mentioned in Hebrews 6:17-20?
   Answer: The immutability of God means that He is
   unchanging in His character and cannot lie. This
   character trait of God provides a sure and steadfast
   anchor for our souls.

2. Why was there a need for the New Covenant according
   to Hebrews 8:6-7?
   Answer: The Old Covenant was not sufficient for the
   salvation of mankind, which necessitated the
   establishment of the New Covenant. The New
   Covenant is built on better promises and offers a
   relationship and fellowship with the Father.

3. How does Hebrews 9:15-17 explain the process of
   receiving the promises of the will?
   Answer: In Hebrews 9:15-17, it is explained that the
   will (New Covenant) was enacted after the death of the
   one who made it (Jesus Christ). Jesus, who rose from
   the dead and ascended to heaven, now mediates as our
   lawyer to ensure we receive the promises written in the
   will.

4. What assurance do believers have regarding their
   victory over the enemy?
   Answer: Believers have the assurance that the Holy
   Spirit, who dwells within them, is greater than the
   enemy in the world. They can walk in deliverance and
   victory, being more than conquerors in Christ Jesus.

5. What does 1 Corinthians 10:13 teach us about facing
   temptations?

Answer: 1 Corinthians 10:13 assures us that no temptation is beyond our ability to endure. God is faithful and provides a way of escape for us to overcome temptations and walk as overcomers.

MORE BOOKS BY CHARLES MORRIS

Look for eBooks (EB), paperbacks (PB), & hardcovers (HC)

1. ***THE FOUR POSITIONS OF THE HOLY SPIRIT***: Beside Us, Within Us, Upon Us, and Filling Us (EB, PB, HC) (2014 02 17; 2021 10 02, 1st, 2nd, & 3rd Editions).
2. ***BORN AGAIN:*** Having a Personal Relationship with God (EB, PB, HC) (2021 07 09, 1st & 2nd Editions).
3. ***THE 10 CHARACTERISTICS OF A SPIRIT-FILLED CHURCH:*** The Spirit-Filled Life Bible Study (EB, PB, 1st Edition).
4. ***THE COVENANT OF SALT:*** Everyone Will be Salted with Fire (EB, PB, HC) (2021 10 03, 1st Edition).
5. ***THE PARABLE OF THE FOUR SOILS:*** The Key to the Mystery of the Kingdom of God. (EB, PB, HC) (2021 06 23, 1st Edition).
6. ***THE FIVE EVIDENCES OF SALVATION:*** How Do I Know That I'm Saved. (EB, PB, HC) (2021 09 10, 1st & 2nd Editions).
7. ***FAITHFUL:*** How Can I Be Faithful to God? (EB, PB, HC) (2021 06 20, 1st & 2nd Editions).
8. ***HOSEA:*** What Does the Book of Hosea Teach Us? (EB, PB, HC) (2021 05 28, 1st Edition).
9. ***PREPARING OURSELVES TO HEAR THE VOICE OF GOD:*** Do You Want to Hear the Voice of God? Book 1 (EB, PB, HC) (2021 06 09, 1st & 2nd Editions).
10. ***FIFTEEN WAYS TO HEAR THE VOICE OF GOD:*** Do You Want to Hear the Voice of God? Book 2. (EB, PB, HC) (2021 06 11, 1st & 2nd Editions).
11. ***THE 24 QUALIFICATIONS OF AN ELDER:*** What Are the Biblical Requirements to Be an Elder? (EB, PB, HC) (2021 07 03, 1st Edition).
12. ***THE BIBLE PROVES ITSELF TRUE*** (EB, PB, HC)

(2021 09 03, 1st Edition).

13. *EXPERIENCING THE BEAUTY OF BROKENNESS:* You Shall Be a Crown of Beauty in the Hand of the Lord, and a Royal Diadem in the Hand of Your God (EB, PB, 1st Edition).

14. *PLACES WHERE GOD AND MAN MEET:* A Guide to Worshipping in Spirit & Truth (EB, PB, HC) (2021 09 25, 1st Edition).

15. *YOUR DASH:* Writing Your Life Journal (PB, 1st & 2nd Edition).

16. *CHART YOUR PATH*: Bible Study Journal (PB, 1st & 2nd Editions).

17. *THE FIVE WITNESSES OF SALVATION:* You Shall Know The By Their Fruit. (EB, PB, HC, 1st Edition).

18. *HOW DO I WRITE A BOOK?* From Passion to Paper to Print (EB, PB, 1st Edition).

19. *HOSEA INTRODUCTION:* Can You Still Hear the Call? (EB, 1st Edition).

20. *HOSEA 1:1-3:* The Divine Command to Marry Gomer. (EB, 1st Edition).

21. *HOSEA 1:4-5:* A Marriage, A Son, and the Promise of Judgment. (EB, 1st Edition).

22. *HOSEA 1:6-7:* A Daughter, an Unfaithful Wife, Heartbreak, and No Mercy (EB, 1st Edition).

23. *HOSEA 1:8-9:* A Son, You Are Not My People, I Am Not Your God. (EB, 1st Edition).

24. *HOSEA 1:10-11:* The Ultimate Promise: Divine Intervention And Restoration. (EB, 1st Edition).

25. *A WILLINGNESS TO BE TAUGHT:* Overcoming The Dull Of Hearing Syndrome. (EB, PB, HC) (2021 12 03, 1st Edition).

26. *LUKE 15:* The Sheep, A Wandering Heart; The Coin, A Careless Heart; The Son, A Rebellious Heart. (EB, PB, 1st Edition).

27. *THE MYSTERY OF LAWLESSNESS UNLEASED.* (EB, PB, HC, 1st Edition).

28. ***THE CHRONOLOGICAL BOOK OF END TIMES:*** 11 Undeniable Prophecies Of The End Times. (EB, PB, HC) (2022 03 16, 1ˢᵗ Edition).
29. ***IS ATHEISM DEAD?***: The Unbelieving Unbelievers Epidemic. Book 1 of the "They Walk Among Us" series. (EB, PB, HC) (2022 03 01, 1ˢᵗ Edition).
30. ***WHEREVER YOU GO TRAVEL JOURNAL:*** The Ultimate Guide To All 50 States. (PB, 1ˢᵗ Edition).
31. ***WHEREVER YOU GO TRAVEL JOURNAL (FOR TEENS):*** The Ultimate Guide To All 50 States. (PB, 1ˢᵗ Edition).
32. ***THE TOPICAL JOURNAL:*** Journal Like A Veteran (PB 1ˢᵗ Edition).
33. ***THE TOPICAL JOURNAL:*** Don't Just Sit There, JOURNAL. For women. (PB, 1ˢᵗ Edition).
34. ***THE TOPICAL JOURNAL:*** Journaling That Impacts Your Life. (PB, 1ˢᵗ Edition). PB 1ˢᵗ Edition.
35. ***WHEREVER YOU GO TRAVEL JOURNAL (FOR THE GUYS):*** The Ultimate Guide to All 50 States. (PB, 1ˢᵗ Edition).
36. ***THE TOPICAL JOURNAL:*** Don't Just Sit There, Journal. For Men. (PB, 1ˢᵗ Edition).
37. ***IS RELIGION DEAD?:*** The Believing Unbelievers Epidemic. Book 2 of the "They Walk Among Us" series. (EB, PB, HC) (2022 06 18, 1ˢᵗ Edition).
38. ***UNLEASHED: Understanding The Mystery Of Lawlessness.*** (EB, PB, HC) (2022 06 26, 1ˢᵗ Edition).
39. ***I FEEL LIKE I'M LOSING MY FAITH:*** How Do I Fix My Faulty Faith? (EB, PB, 1ˢᵗ Edition).
40. ***WE NEED FAITH:*** Faith After Doubt. (EB, PB, HC) (2022 07 25, 1ˢᵗ Edition).
41. ***THE HOLY BIBLE THE KING JAMES VERSION OF THE OLD AND NEW TESTAMENTS -ANNOTATED-:*** (EB 2022 08 06)
42. ***IS CHRISTIAN IMMATURITY DEAD?:*** The Unbelieving Believers Epidemic. Book 3 of the "They

Walk Among Us" series. (EB, PB, HC) (2022 09 02, 1ˢᵗ Edition).

43. ***THE PARABLE OF THE WHEAT AND TARES***: A Guide To Understanding The Kingdom Of God. (EB, PB, HC) (2022 10 08, 1ˢᵀ Edition)

44. ***GO TELL IT ON THE MOUNTAIN:*** The Great Commission; God's Plan To Reach The World. (EB, PB, HC) (2022 11 17 1ˢᵗ Edition)

45. ***THE COST OF DISCIPLESHIP:*** Making Disciples In Turbulent Times; 2 Timothy 2:2 Discipling 101. (EB, PB, HC) (2022 11 23 1ˢᵗ Edition)

46. ***THE POWER OF ONE MORE:*** Mastering The Art Of Leadership. (EB, PB, HC) (2022 12 02 1ˢᵗ Edition)

47. ***THE GOSPEL ACCORDING TO LUKE:*** Luke 15: The Road To Restoration And Fellowship. (EB, PB, HC) (2022 12 19 1ˢᵗ Edition)

48. ***THE GOSPEL ACCORDING TO JESUS:*** Reflections On The Last Teaching Of Jesus: Commentary On John 16. (EB, PB, HC) (2023 01 14 1ˢᵗ Edition)

49. ***I AM:*** More Than Enough In Christ. 180-Day "I AM" Journal. 6 Colors, (EB, PB, HC) (Light Blue, Dark Blue, Gold, Peach, Light Pink, Dark Pink) (2023 01 17)

50. ***SIX ENEMIES OF FAITH:*** Quick Read Bible Study That Will Challenge Your Stinking Thinking. (EB) (2023 01 18)

51. ***SIX DANGEROUS LOVE AFFAIRS:*** God's Crazy Love That Will Challenge Your Stinking Thinking. (EB) (2023 01 20)

52. ***OVERCOMING FEAR:*** How To Live Peaceful In A Fear-Filled World. (EB PB HC) (2023 05 27 1ˢᵗ Edition)

ABOUT THE AUTHOR

CHARLES is passionate about the manifested presence of God, seeing the Father's authentic Biblical leadership taking their position of grace and authority, and working towards seeing true Biblical unity in the Spirit and unity of the faith within the body of Christ. He served the Lord and others in the pastorate for more than 40 years, leading almost 8,000 people to a personal knowledge of the Lord Jesus Christ.

In 2000, Charles founded Raising the Standard International Ministry (RSIM), assisting pastors, spiritual leaders, and the body of Christ to pursue these key objectives.

In 2018, Charles founded Raising the Standard International Publishing (RSIP) to self-publish his books and assist other believers in pursuing their dream of getting the passion of their hearts printed. Charles has written and published more than 50 books.

Charles is an evangelist and church planter known for his uncompromising approach to God's Word without denominational or religious bias. He has the unique ability to use word pictures to paint the truth of God's Word. His uncompromising message instills the virtues of honor and respect for other believers, whether they are in a position of authority, being a peer, or have been entrusted to his shepherding and care. Charles' key message for believers is to die daily to self, embrace the beauty in personal brokenness, and walk in faith and the power of the Holy Spirit.

Made in the USA
Monee, IL
20 September 2024